The Soul's Human Experience

The Soul's Human Experience

Discovering Who You Are, Why You're Here, and What Your Purpose Is

ANNA SCHLINGHOFF

ISBN Paperback #: 979-8-9850877-1-0
ISBN Hardcover #: 979-8-9850877-2-7
ISBN Electronic #: 979-8-9850877-0-3
ISBN Audio #: 979-8-9850877-3-4

Library of Congress#: 2021920997

Portions of this book are works of nonfiction. Certain names and identifying characteristics have been changed.

Printed in the United States of America.

Anna Schlinghoff
hello@annaschlinghoff.com

www.annaschlinghoff.com

For my sister, Allix.

May you always know your light shines bright.

CONTENTS

The Soul's Human Experience

INTRODUCTION

For as long as I can remember, I've been questioning, "Why?" *Why are things the way they are? How did they come to be that way?* I can't help it. My mind is always curious and has a thirst for knowledge and answers. When we are kids, we hear about adults pondering the meaning of life, but it doesn't make any sense—when our only responsibilities are to play, eat, and sleep, we can't understand the question. Adults envy children because they don't have to be accountable for adult problems. After all, children enjoy living in the moment. I wanted to know why we change from being happy kids to unhappy adults—because, all of a sudden, I realized I was an unhappy adult. Then, I understood why people want to know the meaning of life.

What's the answer? Why are we here? Who are we in this big world? Where do we fit in? What are we supposed to be doing? How did we even get here? Why are there no answers to these questions? I didn't know at the time that the Universe and my higher self were leading me on a quest to find out.

*

Everything I'm about to tell you, you already know. You just forgot, so I'm here to remind you. It's an honor to be able to help you remember all of the things you've forgotten. Not things like where you put your car keys, but things like who you really are and why you're really here.

This book is a journey of remembrance and healing. Healing is for everyone. You don't have to have been traumatized (though, unfortunately, most of us have been, whether we realize it or not). You can heal right now, no matter what you've been through, big or small. By reading this book, you are already doing healing work. I'm proud of you already!

*

When I was in my early twenties, I was sitting in a restaurant with a friend one winter night. Over an appetizer of loaded nachos, I asked him, "What do you think the meaning of life is?" At the time, I was confused. I had no clue what I was going to do with my life. When you're that age, for some stupid reason, you're expected to know. There was so much pressure; everyone around me seemed to always be asking, "What are you going to do with your life?" It seemed absurd to declare, "I'm going to devote the next forty years of my life to acquiring knowledge about this industry or that subject."

What was the point? Why did I have to know? What was I doing wrong? The question was bothersome to me, and I didn't have an answer. Maybe if I knew the meaning of life, I'd know what to do with mine ... but my friend didn't have an answer either. After some back-and-forth, I came to the proud conclusion that since there was no solid answer to the question, then there couldn't be a meaning to life at all. A logical conclusion, right? Well, I thought so.

At that time in my life, I didn't believe in anything. I wasn't raised religious, and I wasn't aware of spirituality. In fact, I told my friend, I thought those who believed in religions were not as smart as me because I saw the truth—believing in something that couldn't be backed up with scientific evidence was weakness disguised as hope. The need to "believe" was vital to giving their lives meaning, and without belief, they wouldn't be strong enough to survive the trials of being alive. I thought if they knew the truth I saw so clearly, they simply wouldn't be able to handle it.

There was nothing to believe in as far as I was concerned, because there was no meaning to life. There was no reason for me to think otherwise. I thought I saw right through to the core of this nothingness existence. Accepting my version of the facts made me feel stronger—and better than those who leaned on intangible beliefs to get through their lives. I felt tough. My ego was satisfied (and large). I remember leaving the restaurant that night, feeling like I had all the answers—and no answers at all.

Then, something strange happened. My question about the meaning of life started to haunt me. It would not leave me alone. I found myself thinking about it every day. Clearly, on a deeper level, I did not accept my conclusion of a "meaningless existence." As divine timing would have it, out of the blue a friend told me about an amazing documentary I *had* to watch called, *The Secret*. "It changed my life!" he said and provided no additional context other than, "Just trust me." I was intrigued—and I had nothing else to do. When you're in a low place, anything that promises life-changing results will pique your attention. If only I had a recording of myself watching that documentary. I stared into the screen of my thick, old laptop, barely blinking, eyes wide, jaw hanging open. Maybe that's a bit of an exaggeration, but you get the idea.

The Secret was my wake-up call to something more. It was the first time I'd ever heard that the power of your thoughts can be harnessed to transform your life. Oh, the things I would be able to change just by using my mind! All the things I could have! My head was spinning with ideas about constructing a new life. I was excited, hopeful, and amazed. I felt that I really did know some kind of secret. Why had no one told me about this life hack in over twenty years? I needed to know more, and straight into the deep end of the spirituality pool I dove, head-first.

I became, well, kind of obsessed (and I still am). I was hungry to learn, to get my hands on every spiritual book in existence. I learned there were entire categories for this topic. Spirituality and New Age thinking, why had I never heard of them? Every weekend, I went to the local discount bookstore with my mom. I darted straight for the New Age bookshelf to see what new gems had arrived. Nothing was off-limits; I bought books of all kinds: from self-help to palm reading, Feng Shui to astrology. I was the driest of sponges, desperate to be soaked in all of the available spiritual knowledge. I visited crystal shops, tarot readers, and deepened my yoga practice. I learned more and more (and I decided palm-reading wasn't really for me).

Over the last decade or so, I have found that while excellent and helpful information exists, it exists in a wide array of places and comes from a wide range of teachers and mentors. I found some knowledge here and a different kind there. In some cases, the information was written in such lofty language, it was not accessible to those new to spirituality. There was no single book (that I could find) that gave me the explanations I was looking for in a neat little package with a bow on top. I wanted straightforward answers; a Life User Manual if you will. I wish someone had handed me such a manual years ago (like, way before I saw *The Secret*).

Why is there such mystery surrounding our actual existence? In my ideal world, such a manual would be a children's book and taught in all schools! It would have been comforting for me to have had a solid foundation to stand on as I was going through challenges in life (and before that too).

All this brings me to why I'm writing this book. The spiritual awakening journey is a lot to handle. You go from the wake-up call, to feeling confused, to being overwhelmed, and eventually to (hopefully) sorting it all out. On the other side of my awakening (though it never really stops), I couldn't help but wonder if we even need to go on a spiritual awakening journey. Wouldn't we all be better off if we could make the journey easier? I'm sure some would argue that the spiritual awakening and the subsequent journey is something each of us must go through, like a rite of passage. Personally, I think it would be enormously helpful to the world's population as a whole if we could eliminate some of the mystery and be given answers right from the start. I can't help but think this would transform our world into a more enlightened one and greatly accelerate the expansion of our collective consciousness.

The more people that start waking up to their truths, the more we advance as a collective into a more healed planet. I spent many years searching for answers that resonated with me. When I ultimately came to a place of comfortable understanding, I started to feel personally responsible for not sharing the answers I had found. I am writing this book because I want you to have my answers. Living on Earth is not a test (more on this later), but if it were a test, I'm sharing my answers with you. Your best and fullest life is more possible than you might think!

*

Perhaps you can relate to this scenario: Your alarm goes off, you wake up (half-awake, let's be honest), go to work, work all day, commute home, cook and eat dinner, and consume content for a couple of hours. Before you know it, it's time for bed. You repeat this "Groundhog Day" scenario five days of your week! That's well over half the time in your week that you don't spend on yourself! So many of us are on that unfortunate hamster wheel—and often, we don't know how we got on it in the first place, much less how to jump off. For graduation, or at a certain age, society gifts you with this nice shiny hamster wheel. You hop on enthusiastically (because everyone says you should), and you think, *Hey! This isn't so bad! I kind of like putting on nice clothes and going into an office. They even give me my own desk with my name on it!* That's, of course, assuming a corporate scenario, but a similar scenario could be applied to almost any job. A couple of years go by, and you begin to dread the wheel. Then you find that you straight up despise it, which somehow also sours other aspects of life.

It took me two years of working in the corporate world for any excitement about it to die out completely. Following a repetitive and dull schedule led me to ask myself, *Wait, is this all there is to living? Am I supposed to be happy with this? Do I have to do this almost every day until I retire? By the time I retire, I might not enjoy what I want to do now. Why do I have to wait so long to enjoy my life?* It made no sense. I started to understand the phrase, "Youth is wasted on the young," which depressed me. I felt like I was wasting my life commuting to work in my car, sitting at a desk all day, and then, in the little free time I had, I was too exhausted to do anything but sit on the couch. I couldn't help but think, *There has to be more to life than living like a robot. I can't be alive just to run on my wheel for forty years!* I was determined to find actual answers. Was there another way to live? If it turned out to be true (that this is all there is and I had not been misled after all), I at least needed to know why.

I had followed what American society tells us we should do: go to college, get a job, make money, live happily ever after. Except I wasn't happy at all. I was miserable. I knew I couldn't possibly be the only one living this way; most people are! Pretty much any short personal exchange in an office breakroom will lead one to this conclusion. So, was I the only one dissatisfied enough to question it? Was everyone else just accepting their sad fate? Living on autopilot without question is what I now call "living unawake."

There *is* more to life. Too many of us are walking around totally unawake. For a minority of people, living this way is not bothersome. These individuals are seemingly content with their lives: the end. Weirdly, I envied their life simplicity for a time. I once had a coworker like this. She was in her fifties and had worked a corporate job with a long commute for over twenty-five years. She never complained and seemed happy, no matter what happened. In the face of change, good or bad, she would say, "Oh well," and "It is what it is."

Why couldn't I be satisfied too? Despite these outlier individuals (bless them), I bet at some point most of us have asked the questions, "What am I doing here?", "Who am I, really?", and "If I'm here for a reason, what should I be doing?"

Maybe you've asked yourself these questions out of dissatisfaction, curiosity, or depression. For me, it was the daily monotony, feeling empty inside, and longing for something greater out of life. I suspect some individuals find answers and satisfaction by turning to religion (which, as you know, I'd previously deemed as weakness). I couldn't help but wonder, *Is there still a reason for my existence if I decide not to believe in a God?* One of the things I found attractive about spirituality was that it was another option. It showed me that I didn't need to subscribe to something rigid in order to comprehend the importance of my existence.

I'm happy to say I now know there is more to life than living on autopilot. Even if you are stuck on a 9:00 a.m. – 5:00 p.m. hamster wheel (I still am as I write this!), you can still feel connected to your higher self, the Universe, and your purpose. You can absolutely live your life more authentically and joyfully!

Since making peace with these existential questions, my life has improved dramatically. Feeling connected to my true self and the larger Universe keeps me grounded. On good days, I'm in the flow of life, vibrating in good, high energy, knowing anything is possible. On bad days, the connection and inherent knowing don't let me forget that I matter. I allow myself to feel my feelings and then make my way back to feeling good because I understand the truth of my being.

We are entering a new era of information, a new world even. The population is gradually waking up spiritually, one person at a time. It is my mission to make this information not only accessible but to present it clearly and concisely. I want to remove as much of the mystery as possible and put the puzzle pieces together in a clear picture. I believe it's your right as a human being to know this information. The more people who are informed, the faster we will awaken. This awakening will bring healing, both on an individual level and collectively, to create a better world.

If you've ever wondered who you really are and why you're on this Earth, this book is for you. Think of it as your User Manual for being a human—the one we should all have received at birth, but unfortunately didn't. When I started asking myself these existential questions and searching for answers in books, I didn't understand why there was (seemingly) no clear-cut and comprehensive resource that laid it all out for me. Don't get me wrong, there are many incredible books and resources available on spirituality and how to live your best life, but many of them are niche in nature. That being said, if any of this information doesn't resonate with you, that's okay! Take what does and leave the rest. Just as I needed to find my own answers, the most important thing is that what you believe resonates with you.

A SHORT GLOSSARY OF COMMON SPIRITUAL TERMS

Before we dive in, I think it's essential to do a bit of vocabulary housekeeping. If you're new to the spiritual space, then these terms might be unfamiliar to you. If you're not new here, feel free to apply your own definitions—or ponder mine and perhaps gain a new perspective on an age-old concept.

When I was first finding my way on the spiritual journey, I saw these words everywhere but I wasn't sure what they meant. It seems there's some unwritten rule that you're supposed to know what these terms mean. You might know their literal meanings, but it's a bit deeper in the context of spirituality, and they can be ambiguous. Let's clear this up for good measure, shall we?

Awakening
The process of recognizing your true self and seeing through the illusions we are all taught about this world. It is the mind relinquishing its control over you. As old thoughts and beliefs begin to fall away, new ones in alignment with the highest truth are revealed, bringing about a deeper awareness of your existence and the world you inhabit. Awakening is being present to your thoughts—seeing where they come from and being witness to them. An awakening will allow you to see yourself and the world with new eyes. Awakening can be another word for enlightenment. You can awaken at any moment in your life—you don't need to sit in meditation for days on end. You don't need to be a hermit or a monk. You don't need to be famous or even noteworthy. You can just be *you.*

Freedom
To be free is to see yourself as the limitless entity you are. It is to be free of boundaries, whether those are physical (like the body or worldly containers) or intangible (such as limiting beliefs and fears). The real you is always free from everything your mind might trick you into thinking is reality, but is actually not. At this moment, you are free. You have always been free, and you always will be free.

Fun fact: When I graduated from college I got a tattoo of the word "Freedom" to commemorate my final release from formal education. I had waited almost my entire life to be free of it; I always felt enslaved by schooling. Little did I know then that this word would soon take on a whole other dimension of meaning for me.

Healing

Healing is the process of uncovering, learning about, growing through, and mending wounds, traumas, and old stories. It is working on yourself, being introspective, and recognizing past experiences that have created blockages in the present. Healing is releasing that which has been holding you back and keeping you from living your most fulfilling, aligned life. The healing journey is for everyone. No one has had a perfect life; therefore, we all have "stuff" that has impacted us. No feeling or experience is too small or too big to be healed if it is one that has negatively affected you. Everyone is capable of doing healing work on themselves, so you *can* free yourself from your "stuff."

DISCLAIMER

A quick note on religion and terminology: This book is for both the religious and non-religious. It is non-denominational. Since I am not religious, I use neutral language to refer to divinity. For example, God, Source, the Universe, the Greater Consciousness, and the Divine are all examples that refer to a Greater Conscious Being. Please feel free to change my words and substitute language that resonates with you. This book is universal; it is for everyone.

WHO YOU REALLY ARE

All About Souls

Reminding You of Who You Are

When someone asks who you are, what do you say? Do you give them your name, age, roles, or titles? None of these things are actually you. It's okay if you've forgotten who you are because you're about to be reminded. Knowing and understanding the truth of who you are will give you a solid foundation to stand on and keep you anchored in the chaos of life. When things get tough, you'll stay grounded—outside influences won't shake you. Other people won't be able to convince you to be what they think you should be. Why? Because you will know, deep down, what is true. What is true is this:

You are a soul with a temporary human body.

You, soul, are eternal.

You are a piece of the Universe itself.

You are the energy of conscious love.

You are an immortal soul currently existing in this time with a human body and personality. You are the Universe individualized. The Universe is intelligent by design, therefore you are a piece of this conscious energy. You are the energy of conscious love manifesting as you, right now. That's it. *It's simple.*

So, what is the soul, anyway? The soul is your spiritual, intangible, eternal, energetic being. It's your core essence, the part of you that transcends time and space. The soul is expressed as the spirit, the light, the energy body, the higher self—or you can call it by whatever term suits you. However you label it, your soul is a piece of the Universe currently expressing itself in your human body. It was with you before you were born, and it will be with you after you depart this mortal container.

The soul joins with the body sometime before birth and parts with it at the moment we die. The latter has been corroborated by people who have had Near-Death Experiences (NDEs). They speak of floating above their bodies, unable to talk or touch anything but knowing what is happening. Who is it that has this disembodied awareness of physical reality? It is the soul—that part of us that belongs to the greater, loving energy source that is the Universe.

Yes—you are a piece of the Universe. You are the Universe mirroring itself back to itself, celebrating its own expansion. *As Above, So Below.* Your body and soul coexist beautifully, manifested as you, here on planet Earth right now. You are conscious love. Everything is energy, as confirmed by modern physics. The energy of the Universe is pure love, therefore you are pure love energy that can think, feel, and be aware in this physical plane. *How beautiful is that?*

*

For thousands of years, the soul was thought to be part of the human body. Numerous ancient Greek philosophers, for example, had differing opinions about the nature of the soul and its relationship to the physical world. Some early thinkers pinpointed its physical location as the brain. Others believed the soul was in the blood; still, others thought it was bound up in the stars.

While the predictions have been varied, it's an idea that has persisted throughout human history. This inherent knowing that there is more to us than meets the eye.

For as long as human beings have existed, we have yearned to know the meaning of life. Most religions and cultures acknowledge the existence of the human soul. Throughout our past, we have sought wisdom that proves we are a part of something greater than our earthly selves, regardless of our specific beliefs. The existence of souls does not have to be identified with any particular faith, philosophy, or culture; it can be neutral.

*

For the longest time, no one told me I was a soul in a body. This was a completely foreign concept to me—until I started my deep dive into spirituality. It's possible I was living under a rock—sure, I'd heard phrases like "feeding the soul," "warming the soul," "selling your soul," "speaking to the soul," and "soul searching." I knew the soul was, supposedly, some deep part of me, but I wasn't clear on exactly what it was, what its purpose was, or why it existed—if, in fact, it did. When I finally understood what it was and that I was a soul living with a human body, I found myself wanting to shout this knowledge to every person I passed on the sidewalk.

Hi! Do you know that you're a soul in a body? You're a soul in a body! And you're a soul in a body!

It was my Oprah moment (in my head).

Every person has a right to know who they really are (if they don't already). Since I didn't know for such a long time, I couldn't be the only one—surely not everyone was aware of their soul and exactly what it means to be one. (I wish we all were!) It frustrates me that this is not a more mainstream idea. If you don't understand who you are, it can be disorienting, confusing, and heavy to exist here on Earth. It's time to talk about this! More and more people are discovering their true nature, but we have a ways to go before everyone on the planet knows this truth—and everyone has a right to know.

We are spiritual beings having a human experience. You're already a part of the Universe. You don't need to do anything. You're a one-of-a-kind energetic fingerprint, perfect exactly as you are. You don't need to change anything about yourself to know this. Give yourself permission to embrace this idea of yourself fully, including anything about yourself you might initially see as flawed. See yourself instead as a piece of the beautiful Universe. You are the essence of love shining as only you can.

All Souls Are Connected to the Universe and Each Other

The pulse of the Universe runs through you.

Being a piece of the Universe means you are always connected to it and to every part of it. In the loving Universal space inside you, you already have all the answers that have ever and will ever exist because universal consciousness has all the answers. Since you are always connected, this knowledge is always available to you whenever you are seeking support. You can tap into this constant connection for any want or need, big or small. The knowledge and strength of universal consciousness are yours to use at any time, and acknowledging this connection is the first step of getting into flow with it. To access it, get quiet with your soul. Listen, and feel for any subtle intuitions, sensations, or feelings. Communication comes in many ways, so stay open and continue to practice. The Universe and our souls are always communicating with us. However, we have become good at automatically tuning them out. The more you tune in, the stronger the connection becomes.

We are all made of the same energy, we are all connected, and we are all one—one with each other and one with the Universe. Everyone and everything is an extension of you, and you of it. The power of the Universe is everywhere. It is in every person and every thing. Before I understood this on a spiritual level, I understood it scientifically; we are all made up of the same star stuff, as astrophysicist Carl Sagan famously explained. (I'm not just a spirituality enthusiast, but a space enthusiast too.) The elements that make up our physical bodies are the same elements that can be found in the stars of our Universe. When stars die by way of a supernova explosion, these elements are ejected into the Universe. Over billions of years, these scattered elements gather into form and become objects, such as planets, and ultimately, they created us, humans. This makes you the same as your friend, your neighbor, a stranger, the tree, the mountain, the ocean, the cloud, the bird. You get the idea. We are all made of the same common building blocks. We are literally made from parts of the Universe.

Seeing from this place of sameness instead of difference creates a dramatic shift in how we view our place in the world. When we recognize that we are all the same, we can have greater compassion for each other automatically—and having a greater sense of compassion brings more love into the world. As a society, we can strive to be better in this way. You are already whole and complete. You are divine perfection right now. By accepting yourself, you accept others and vice versa—by accepting others, you accept yourself.

I once had a boss I disliked. I saw him as different than me; I imagined I would never treat others the way he treated his team. He was unfair, unkind, and not a good leader in my opinion. I was always nice to him despite that, but my job was a struggle. I was forever trying to prove myself, whereas it seemed my coworkers received praise and promotions without any effort. It seemed utterly unfair and made me dread going to work.

I put myself through this struggle for years. Finally, desperate, I said to the Universe, "Please help me to see my boss another way." I truly wanted to. The toxicity and negativity had become overwhelming, and if this didn't change things then I was going to leave. Slowly, I began to find more compassion for him—I shifted my perspective from seeing him not only as a boss but as a fellow human being, a person with his own faults and problems. To others, he was also a father, a husband, a neighbor, and of course, he was a fellow soul. Maybe he wasn't so different from me after all. I chose to see this aspect of him rather than the things that bothered me. The negative energy slowly began to dissipate. Once I'd made a habit of this, things started to change noticeably. The hostility diminished. Then a couple of months later, out of the blue, he gave me a promotion and a raise. It was a miracle.

You, too, can make these shifts. You only have to be willing to try. Willingness opens the door to possibility. Seeing the soul in others recognizes them as you while also seeing both of you as the same universal energy. You must be willing to stop putting energy into your current ideas about others and instead put your energy into seeing their soul—their light. By shifting your energy, you shift the outcome. It creates space for change and tells the Universe, "I am willing to shift the way I view this person."

It may take time and practice to get over your initial feeling of resistance. For a long time, I was not even remotely interested in seeing my boss differently. That seemed radical. I didn't think I could change my opinion of him, and I didn't want to. Frankly, in my view, he did not "deserve" to be seen as anything other than his negative actions. So why should I try? But thinking that way wasn't beneficial, so I was willing to try, just a little. A little turned into a lot. A year later, my perception of him had changed dramatically, from dislike and disgust to—dare I say it—likability. He had changed too—he was kinder, more patient, and understanding. I'm not taking credit for changing him, but I can't help wonder if my shift in perspective had an impact on him at an energetic level. Either way, it was amazing.

Initially, it might feel as if the other person is not worthy of having their faults overlooked. This practice is not about them or excusing any of their faults and wrongs. We don't have to forgive, forget, or excuse in order to see the light in someone. These two things don't have to go together. This is about you and your peace and freedom. Keep that in mind, and the practice becomes easier.

*

I believe this way of seeing others with compassion and oneness is essential for bringing about a bigger change in our world. Imagine if we could all practice this—there would be less road rage, less rudeness, more patience, and more joy. It starts with you, and you can start today.

You can make a difference in shifting the global consciousness.

When you have compassion for just one person, that positive energy gets put into space and directed toward them. They may feel it (whether consciously or unconsciously), and in turn, be kinder to their family, their coworkers, and all the people they come in contact with. You may think you helped just one person, but actually, your good energy will multiply and touch the lives of many more people. That's how you help the collective—one person at a time, supporting them to feel better and understand more about who they are. Hopefully, they will teach by example and do the same.

You Are Not Your Body

As we have established, you are not your body; you just happen to exist with one right now. The spiritual text, *A Course in Miracles,* says, "I am not my body. I am free." You are not your personality or emotions. You are not your titles or roles. You are a piece of the infinite Universe and its pure, boundless love. Your body is a container, a vehicle. Just as you cannot drive on the road without a car or bike, and astronauts can't walk outside the International Space Station without a spacesuit, you can't exist as a human on this planet without a body. The body is a temporary home. If you take away the body, what remains is who you truly are: your eternal soul-self.

Your soul will outlive your body. It has existed in prior bodies, and it will go on to live with future bodies as well, which is not to say that you should disregard your body. In fact, it's the complete opposite. Treating your body with care, respect, and love shows your soul care, respect, and love. Similarly, you (hopefully) take care of your literal home, for it is a reflection of who you believe yourself to be. Taking care of your soul's home is essential for its nurturing and for the optimal overall human experience. After all, that's why we're here, to express ourselves in human form.

Your body deserves your kindness, love, and respect. Sure, your body might need troubleshooting from time to time; it's not perfect. Listening to your body, honoring its needs, and providing it with quality nourishment and movement is good for both your body and your soul. You don't need to go out and detox, do a fast, or sit on a mountaintop meditating; just honor what feels good to you. What makes your body feel best? Do more of that. How do you treat your body now? How can you treat it moving forward?

I try to remember to thank my body for all the things it allows me to do. I'm grateful that it gives me the ability to go on daily walks, read books, and taste and eat food. When treated with appreciation and kindness, your body will reciprocate, giving you good health and vitality.

We are here to recognize the soul within the body, to live in our body from a soul-centered place so that we can have this earthly adventure. To embrace the soul and the body as the same is such a beautifully unique human experience. Your body is the only home your soul will have in this lifetime. No matter what your physical circumstance is, you are still breathing and you are alive; you are supposed to be here in this moment. And remember, your body is not who you really are at the deepest level.

You might be wondering, *But my physical body is real. How can I not be my body? I feel pain if I touch something hot. If I get cut, I bleed.* Your body is real to the extent that the Earth is real. The physical body can feel and be harmed, so it is real in that sense. But it is not real to the extent that it is a temporary experience and not part of your soul. You don't need to *identify* with (or as) your body on a spiritual level. You are physically with your body right now, but your soul is free. The mind is part of the physical body, and you can pause and step outside the confines of the mind at any time. Therefore, you are free.

The body you had when you were a child is not the same body you had as a teenager, and it's not the one you have as an adult—the body changes. The world around you changes. But the real you, the soul, is always there, unchanging; consciously aware of it all. Intuitively, we have a deep knowing of our soul's existence. Your soul (the real you) has been witness to all the thoughts, emotions, and physical world experiences you have had up to this point in your life. Your soul is the place of your higher consciousness and awareness. You exist eternally without your body, without your thoughts and emotions. Your body is finite, bound by earthly rules of chronological, linear time. This is in contrast to the eternal or non-existent time by which your soul lives. As human beings, it can be difficult for us to grasp this abstract alternative concept of time. In outer space, time has strange behavior and can bend, contort, and even appear to stop. At the quantum level, time may be an emergent phenomenon or not exist at all. The concept of time is a mysterious one that physicists are still researching. Whatever the case, our normalized perception of a separate past, present, and future is not as real as it seems. If time is not as we perceive it to be, then perhaps our entire reality is not as we observe it either.

The Balancing Act

When people speak of becoming enlightened, it seems they speak of living in a state that has transcended their humanness in some way. We are curious about (and sometimes chase after) enlightenment, because as human beings we are often miserable. On one end of the spectrum we have our human, ego-driven experience; on the other end we have the experience of the enlightened soul. Before we awaken we live at the ego end of the spectrum. When we awaken and our spiritual practice becomes a habit, we live from the soul. While neither is good nor bad, nor wrong nor right (nor is one better than the other), finding a balance is the key to living a fulfilling life.

Living from your soul self is phenomenal. Here, you are free and joyous—nothing can touch you in this place of peace. Living from a human place, on the other hand, means being immersed in the world you came to explore, with all its rawness and realness. So, how do we balance the soul with the body and get the best of both worlds? By recognizing the soul and allowing it to play freely in the humanness. To only live from the transcended soul would be to renounce the very thing we came to experience. To only live from the human end would be to lack depth and understanding, and to never know true freedom.

The spiritual journey provides invaluable tools to navigate our time here. It can be difficult to enjoy being a human being without a reference point. It would be pretty hard for a soul to enjoy being human without having a physical body in this world. Upon first consideration it might seem as though the body and the soul are like oil and water, two complete opposites that do not mix. However, equipped with knowledge of how each operates and experience of each, they can be emulsified beautifully. To be a human being and to be a soul at the same time is the sweet spot. Herein lies the beauty and balance of this world—walking the fine line between human and soul. You may wander to one side for a while. You may wander way off course! But true alignment is a healthy balance of the two. That doesn't mean everyone's line is the same. For one person, it may be more comfortable to walk further in the spiritual. For another, it might feel better to live a little more on the human side. What feels good to you?

The Soul Wants to be Recognized – Your Sacred Glow

Once I became spiritually awake, I realized that it would be easier to live as a human being if this spiritual knowledge were common knowledge taught to us at a young age. After we are born, the awareness of our soul fades like a distant memory or a dream. Without a remembering, we live our entire lives believing that we are only physical beings in a physical world. The more heavily we rely upon the physical, the farther we move from our soul connection.

These days, in our modern society, we live in disconnect, despite the irony that the internet connects us all in an instant. We seem to care more about our perception on social media than about our planet or our spiritual connection. But as we continue to spiritually awaken, society will change. You can be a part of this change by sharing this message and shining your light. Your light is the expression of your soul. Never underestimate the power of your light.

When one person shines their light on others, those people feel inspired to share their light as well. It creates a ripple effect that grows exponentially. We could all use a little more love and compassion. Be the light of love that you are and shine brightly.

Whenever you see another human, say to yourself, "I honor your light." Even if your eyes can't physically see this light, we are luminous. Our human eyes are limited. I imagine we would be overstimulated if we were able to see wavelengths beyond the ranges of the visible electromagnetic spectrum. Just because this sight wasn't meant for our human eyes does not mean it doesn't exist.

The Feeling of a Soul and Love of the Universe

I once had an incredible encounter and the privilege of experiencing a soul's "physical" feeling. Of course the soul is not tangible, but it is made of energy, and energy can be felt.

My sophomore year in college, some of my friends threw a Halloween party. A friend (I'll call him Matt), also planning on attending the party, told me that he had found the most amazing costume. "I'm going to show up to the party as a giant, oversized green crayon," he said. "But don't tell anyone, it's a surprise."

The party came and went; everyone had a great time. But Matt never showed up, which was odd—he had been so excited to show everyone his costume. None of us thought much of it. We knew he was working late that night. Early the following day, my phone rang over and over again. Finally, I got out of bed and answered groggily. It was a mutual friend of Matt and mine. His voice shaking, he told me that on his way to the party Matt had been in a bad car accident and had passed away. He'd been just five minutes from the party and in an instant a driver under the influence took his life. I was in shock. Time seemed to stop. It was one of those heavy moments that's imprinted in your memory forever.

A week or so after his passing, I had a dream I'll never forget. Except it didn't feel like a dream at all, it felt real. To this day, it is the most vivid, realistic dream I've ever had. Matt and I were standing across from one another in an empty space, a space of silence and nothingness. I was aware that he was no longer alive in the physical sense. He smiled, and I stepped forward to give him a great big hug. The instant my arms touched him, an electricity of the purest, most joyful, loving, and ecstatic energy engulfed my entire body. It was intense and breathtaking in the most beautiful way. We hugged for a matter of seconds. That was it—I woke up.

The intensity of the experience and the comfort it brought me were incredibly overwhelming. The power of soul energy is immense. At that point in my life, I was still not a spiritual person. I had no preconceived notions about souls or "the other side." Now I know that this was what many would call "a visitation." He had wanted to show me he was okay "over there." He gave me the beautiful gift of experiencing what a soul feels like and what pure universal energy must feel like as well.

I am forever grateful for this gift. Not only did it give me the closure I needed to say goodbye to my friend, but it gave me something else—proof. I didn't recognize this until years later. But when I recalled this experience, I knew it was the validation I'd been looking for—that there is more to our existence; that we each have a soul that is part of something greater, and that is the pure love of the Universe.

How Can I Be Sure I Have a Soul?

You might be thinking, *Are you sure I have a soul?* Yes, I am sure. You wouldn't be here if you didn't. There are no soulless bodies walking around on Earth. Every living being here has a piece of the Universe within them. Your existence is no accident. To be connected to your highest self is to be connected with universal energy. It's to be in the flow, to feel supported, and to know that you matter. To be disconnected feels hopeless, pointless, and joyless. Sadly, a lot of us can relate to the latter emotions as being all too common. Whether we realize it or not, our existence is no accident. Even those of us who have a daily spiritual practice of some kind (yes, it's a lifelong practice!) can slip into these frames of mind. It's okay. It happens. Part of the practice is knowing how to pull yourself out of a disconnect and get back into the flow.

But it's not just ordinary people who are disconnected and need to find their way back to flow. There are different levels of disconnection, and most of us are just a little out of alignment. What about the high school bully, the thief, even the murderer? These individuals are disconnected from their soul and their universal Source. They strayed so far off track their free will took over in a negative way. They don't see their home base anymore, and their soul-disconnect traps them in an energy of fear. They are no longer living in the energy of Source (which is self-perpetuating love). They are caught in a low energy of fear (which is also self-perpetuating). These individuals are some of our most difficult teachers. They serve as examples of what can happen with disconnect. When we encounter them they can strengthen us (if we allow ourselves to respond in this way).

Soulmates

We all want to know if we have a soulmate. It seems from a young age we all hope to find ours one day. But a soulmate is probably not what you think it is. The word "soulmate" is a widely misunderstood term. A soulmate is another soul we are drawn to because they help us awaken to our truths and help us grow our light. Often, this soul will act as a mirror, revealing what needs healing within us. When the time is right, they act as a catalyst in our growth by forcing us to face and accept things we might not otherwise. If it isn't revealed, it can't be healed! Soulmates push us out of our comfort zone so we can evolve for our highest good. This person (contrary to what Hollywood moviemakers would have you believe) is not always a romantic partner. It could be a sibling, a parent, a friend, even a teacher. You will likely feel connected to this person from the first time you meet—it may seem as if you have met before or have known each other for a long time.

We expect a soulmate relationship to be easy, loving, and perfect. While some souls *do* support our expansion through tremendous love and encouragement, others might teach us in a more abrasive and challenging way. In the latter case, a bit of friction might be required to reveal what we need to heal in ourselves, which allows us to clearly see the wound. Sometimes we have to be forced to look at ourselves. Both experiences stem from love, even the rough ones. You are likely helping to expand your soulmate in some way, just as they are helping you. Soulmate relationships are on purpose—your soulmate is part of your journey, and you are part of theirs.

Think of all the souls on this planet. The ones you are close to are on purpose. People don't come into each other's lives by accident, soulmate or not. To be clear, it may be that your partner is your soulmate! Yes, you have at least one soulmate (and likely several) who will come into your life when you're ready. Soulmates might come and go depending on what we need in life at that time. You can have more than one in a lifetime. The point is, we think we have to go on this endless search for our soulmate, but we don't, because it's not about what we think it is. It doesn't make you any less valuable as a soul in this world if you don't have a partner. Don't worry if you feel you haven't encountered any of yours yet. It's not a race!

As far as the romantic partnership aspect goes, it's okay to want a partner if the reasoning is in alignment with your highest good. A soulmate is not someone who will complete you or make you feel whole. You are already complete and whole. These feelings can only come from within. A soulmate is not meant to bring you happiness or a perfect relationship. Happiness will never come from anywhere outside of you. To search outside ourselves for what already lies within will lead only to disappointment. Rather, your soulmate complements you, but only you can complete you. If completeness is what you're searching for in a soulmate, then the person you seek is you.

WHY YOU ARE REALLY HERE – PART I

How Did I Get Here, Anyway?

You are here because you chose to be here.
And you chose to be here to have a
spectacular experience.

Welcome, Earthling

Your soul came here with a plan to live a remarkable life. That's right, your human existence wasn't a random chance or coincidence; it was a deliberate choice. You came here to experience being human! You came to feel love, to feel pain, to taste chocolate, to pet dogs, to smell fresh rain, and to breathe fresh air (just to name a few human sensations). These things don't exist for us as souls because the soul world (or spirit world) is made up of intangible energies. It's a place of infinite love that is without physicality. As a spirit wanting to incarnate, it must sound appealing to imagine experiencing all the experiential things on Earth. The true challenge is to enjoy it. We get so caught up in our daily tasks, monotony, and negativity, we forget why we came here in the first place. Honestly, it is about continuously finding enjoyment in the small moments of life—and savoring them.

In the depths of my existential crisis, I screamed (in my head and to the Universe) *I didn't ask to be born! I'm a prisoner brought here against my will and I hate it!* I didn't understand I had been chosen to be here. When I first heard that we chose our Earth experience, I immediately rejected it. *No way*, I thought. *I would never have chosen this life. I'm straight up not having a good time and if I could have chosen, then I'm stupid for not choosing fortune or fame.* But the truth is, there's a good reason I didn't choose those things—and a good reason we all don't choose that kind of incarnation.

Choosing the seemingly perfect body or the perfect life does not determine happiness, satisfaction, or success because these can be found in any body and any situation. Just because you have the ideal body, fortune, or fame does not mean you will be happy and have a perfect life. It's easy for us to think the grass is greener on the other side of the fence and that our life would have been easier or better if we had chosen differently. Not so! We've all heard about people who, despite "having it all," are seriously unhappy. Your soul doesn't care about ego-driven things like appearance, money, or recognition. Your soul cares about experiences. *We didn't come here to live the perfect life in a perfect body!* That's not the point. The point is to up-level humanity. In other words, we are here to further humanity's development by increasing our capacity to give and receive love. We achieve this through teaching each other how to be better human beings. The body we choose is perfect for what we plan to teach in this life. The family we choose is perfect. The life plan we choose is perfect. It's all divinely orchestrated with the mission in mind.

For those that do end up with fame or fortune, it just so happens that those are the circumstances required for their part in this incarnation. The events of your life are no accident; they are purposeful choices your soul made as it laid out your life's plan. Perhaps your soul decided this was the lifetime it would teach forgiveness. So, your soul set up scenarios (with other souls as the players) where wrongs would be done to you that you would later need to forgive. Perhaps your soul wanted to teach courage, so it planned to encounter fearful events that you would need to rise above. The possibilities are endless. Practically every concept is one we could all improve on. Sometimes, from the perspective of our human experience, it is hard to accept that our souls would lay out such difficult paths for us. But the perspective from the soul is different; it sees the bigger picture and what it needs to teach in order for humanity to expand. So, your soul mixed up a perfect blend for you to cultivate the ideal circumstances in which you could experience this expansion, and so you could shine in the way your soul planned.

This probably isn't your first Earth rodeo. It's highly likely you've been here before as other bodies with different personalities. You may have been here once or twice, hundreds, or even thousands of times. A younger soul may have come to Earth a few times, while older souls have been here many times. Can you intuitively sense which one you are?

Why would a soul choose to keep coming back to Earth? Because Earth is addictive, I'm sure! I imagine there's nothing quite like it. Think of all the possibilities that life on Earth could be. For example, a soul may want to experience all different genders, economic classes, careers, friend and family groups, countries and cultures, or appearances and personalities. The combination of options is infinite. It sounds tempting to try out as many as possible, doesn't it? Besides, there's a lot of work to be done here, and luckily a lot of us volunteers to help accomplish it.

The fact that you are reading this book means you chose Earth. So, pause for a moment and cultivate a sense of appreciation and wonder at your decision to be here. *Wow!*

Now, let's talk about what your other options might have been. You could have decided simply to go nowhere. According to the work of hypnotherapist and regressionist Dr. Michael Newton, a soul is never forced to do anything or go anywhere. It is always our soul's choice. Maybe the idea of living as a human being does not sound appealing to some souls. Of course, *you* didn't think so because you're here in a body. When you make your transition back to the spirit world, maybe you'll end up spending the equivalent of fifty Earth years hanging out there. Or maybe you'll want to come right back here. You may also have had an option to incarnate on other planets or worlds very different from our own. Individuals who have undergone past life regressions and life between lives regressions have spoken about these other places and their choice to go to them. These other worlds might be places of energy-only, or they may be entirely different forms of existence (such as a water world). It's difficult for our brains to comprehend what this might be like since we know only our human existence. These regressed individuals seem to overwhelmingly agree that otherworld incarnations are less challenging than an Earth incarnation. Earth incarnations are for those souls who don't shy away from a challenge—and this means you. Be proud of this choice! You are brave, and you are here on purpose.

You probably wouldn't go to a concert and spend the entire evening in the venue's lobby. It's kind of like that. If you can accept that you're here of your own free will, you can start viewing your life from a different perspective—one of appreciation, empowerment, wonder, adventure, and enjoyment. Jump in and embrace life! We came here for a reason—let's get the most out of it!

Your Soul's Plan

There is an overall design for you during your time here, and you are part of your planning team. Let this empower you. It can be easy to feel helpless about what life throws at us, but nothing is a mistake. You are not a victim or prisoner here (as I used to firmly believe I was). You and your spiritual guides selected the themes for your life. You came here fully understanding and agreeing to what you would likely encounter. When you view your life from the perspective of your higher self you will realize we all came here to teach one another, so we can evolve into better human beings over time (while at the same time having fun!). We help each other because we are all one.

The life you're living right now is part of your soul's plan. We choose our family, our major experiences, our bodies, even our names. Your selections will draw to you the experiences you wish to have. Everyone in your "circle" planned in advance and agreed to the soul work you would do together. Just as you chose your parents, they chose you. You may also have chosen to parent a child. Each relationship benefits the soul in some way. Your chosen teaching themes are outlined in your soul's plan. These are all individual to you.

But not every single thing in your life is destined by the Divine. For example, what you have for lunch or what kind of car you drive are likely matters of free will and the ego. But overall, you selected, on purpose, certain significant ways or themes in which you would be challenged—and these challenges might rock your world. They will make you ask difficult questions and face certain fears so you come out on the other side able to teach and help others. If you're uncomfortable or dissatisfied with who you are or where you are, congratulations. Discomfort is the birthplace of growth. It's a chance to learn, expand, and level up. At the same time, it's a place to play. As humans, we have the unique capacity to experience great joy. It's not all bad, not even close! You will be stretched, purposely, for greater receiving. Sometimes it will be in pleasant ways and other times in more demanding ways. Will you allow it? Will you embrace it?

I believe that one of my themes of this lifetime is teaching others to remember the truths of their existence. In order to teach this, I had to learn the material myself because I couldn't teach what I didn't know. It required me to experience firsthand challenges that relate to this teaching. I questioned. I felt despair. But I came out of it with knowledge and experience to pass along. I am transferring that knowledge to you now. This is not my only teaching theme, however. I'm sure there are other themes outlined in my soul plan. I'm already aware of some of them, and it's likely there are several more I'm not yet aware of. I feel excited to find out about them later in my life. I welcome them because they are further opportunities for me to expand and help others.

So, what is the point of teaching? Right now, we as human beings have a long way to evolve. Our world is still largely fear-based. Through teaching, we help each other to better ourselves. With each expanded human comes a more expanded world. Fear will be replaced with love. Humanity's larger evolution depends on this continuing practice.

Often, the themes we've outlined in our soul plans are purposefully challenging because it's a way to get our attention. This is just part of the journey. While the teaching themes are laid out, we can get there in different ways. As in, there's sometimes more than one way to solve a math problem yet still arrive at the same answer. The meandering is part of the fun.

Know that you are a unique and valuable teacher on this planet. You have something to offer that only you can share—even if you don't yet recognize what it is.

The Illusion – You're Abroad

While in university I always wanted to study abroad, especially as a foreign language major. Financial constraints and my fear of the unknown stopped me from ever committing to it. When I was a semester away from graduating, I experienced serious FOMO and regret about not having done it. So, after graduation, instead of studying abroad, I took a job as an au pair in Germany. I packed my life into a suitcase and moved to Berlin. I had never been to Germany but was determined to have an international experience before it was "too late" (a.k.a., entering the working world for the next forty-plus years). Living on planet Earth is a lot like going on an international trip away from your actual home: the world of souls.

Everything is different here.
You learn from scratch how to adapt and navigate the experience.
The experiences are all new, like viewing

the world through the eyes of a child seeing something for the first time.
You are homesick at times, questioning if coming here was the right choice.
You will learn and grow a lot.
It will be the experience of a lifetime.

The life we're experiencing now is so real to us. We're completely immersed in it; it's all around us. Purposefully, that realness is by design, but the truth is it's an illusion. I'm not trying to discount your abroad experience. Just because it's an illusion doesn't mean it doesn't matter. It does matter because we're living in it—illusion or not. It's just that Earth is not your true home. It's a temporary home, just as the body is temporary. Nothing here is truly real; everything is a construct of the collective mind. What *is* real is the universal energy of love—the same energy that exists in you. If you prefer a more scientific approach, as the great Albert Einstein once said: "Reality is merely an illusion, albeit a very persistent one."

Ultimately, I was let go from my position as an Au Pair after just a few months (I'll tell you why later), and sadly, the family and I didn't part on the best of terms. I don't regret it though. I would do it over again in a heartbeat. Overall, I enjoyed the experience and the adventure, and in a short time, I expanded a lot as a person. I don't want you to regret your Earth experience. It can be optimized to be the best time possible if we have the proper knowledge and tools. I imagine this is a similar scenario for repeat incarnations. Some incarnations are better than others, and perhaps (sometimes) we don't leave on the best terms. But we don't regret the choices we made, and we'd do it again (and we do).

We are travelers on a cosmic journey,
stardust, swirling and dancing in the
eddies and whirlpools of infinity.
Life is eternal.
We have stopped for a moment to encounter each
other, to meet, to love, to share.
This is a precious moment.
—Paulo Coelho, The Alchemist

Your Other Rights as a Human on Planet Earth

Miracles. Miracles are your right! They occur naturally and are ready to come to you now—if you're willing to let them in. The spiritual text, *A Course in Miracles,* says, "You are entitled to miracles." So often we equate miracles with extraordinary God-like acts. But a miracle isn't always a huge change in circumstance.

A miracle is a shift in perspective.
A miracle is a small win.
A miracle is deciding for love instead of fear.

We are entitled to miracles because miracles are written in the natural language of the Universe. Miracles are a form of love, and since the Universe is eternal love (as are we), we are worthy of miracles. Miracles are happening all the time, and there are more than enough to go around for everyone.

You might be wondering *how* to access them. You already have everything you need to access miracles. The power of miracles is the same power that runs through you. All you need to do is ask and expect to receive them. The miracle you wish for is not unreasonable—it's easy for the Universe to provide miracles. To the Divine, one miracle is not more difficult than another. Receiving miracles is natural for everyone. Your openness to receiving is the determining factor. You might even practice physically opening your arms wide to get into receiving mode. No, it's not too good to be true. When we view miracles from an energetic perspective, we can understand that there is an infinite supply. So, know that you are worthy of miracles and that they will unfold for you effortlessly and regularly.

I have a personal mantra that I say to myself every morning when I wake up. "I radiate light everywhere I go. I am always supported, and miracles come to me easily and often." This puts me into alignment for the day, reminds me of my truth, and reminds me that the Universe is always on my side. Feel free to adopt this mantra as your own, or craft one that suits you so you too can know that you are the light of the Universe who is supported and worthy of miracles.

Support

The Universe and your spirit guides are always on your side, working for your highest good every day. You can call on them anytime and for anything, no matter how big or small. As a way of staying in communication with my guides, I often ask for a sign. If it's not already part of your practice, I encourage you to try asking for a sign. It can be anything you like—ask your spirit guides to bring you a feather, a coin, a word, or an image, just to let you know they are with you. Let yourself be surprised!

Once I request a sign (usually in my head), I am open to receiving it in an unexpected way. For example, at a time when I was doubting myself and feeling alone, I asked my guides to show me a blue butterfly, which is the sign I use most often for communication with them. I hadn't seen one in quite some time, and I needed confirmation they were still around. I put the request in and released it, then went on my daily walk through my neighborhood. About ten minutes into my walk, I turned a corner and saw the most extravagant yard decorations at the house in front of me. The small front courtyard was decorated for a birthday, and there were two giant, blue butterfly sculpture decorations. I couldn't believe what I was seeing! The sheer size of these butterflies made tears well up in my eyes. Message received!

Signs aren't always given so boldly or obviously. They are more often understated. Guides can be very creative, and we are never alone or forgotten, ever. Each of us has a group of spirit guides who are energetic beings that have chosen to be paired with us and to assist us in our earthly journey. They are ready and willing 24/7 to help and guide us. They want to help! It's their job, after all. Despite this, guides don't interfere unless they are asked to do so, or when they deem it absolutely necessary. Otherwise, to interfere without our asking would be an intrusion on our free will—a foundation of our experience here. Therefore, their help is most effective when we ask for it. This sends out a clear signal and clearance for them to step in.

You can ask for help through prayer, intention, or whatever way feels right to you. Your spirit guides will hear you and respond, usually in gentle, subtle ways such as giving you signs or symbols or creating synchronicities. I like to call on my spirit guides daily for protection, guidance, and anything else I might need support with. For example, if I'm feeling down, I might ask a guide to bring laughter into my day. If I'm stuck on a problem, I will ask my guides for direction and assistance. Their communication can come in many forms—through sudden inspirational thoughts; by unexpectedly becoming aware of something you hadn't seen before (though maybe it's been right in front of you all along); receiving a phone call or email from someone who has the answer to your problem; seeing a social media post that contains the perfect information at the perfect time. If you are open to receiving help from the spirit world in different ways, you will receive it.

You might be wondering why guides don't give more straightforward or specific answers and direction. *Why don't they offer more than signs and synchronicities? Why don't they tell me exactly what I should do?* They often gently nudge us and communicate with us through signs and synchronicities because it's our language. These are messages we can understand. Their job is not to tell us what to do, it's to help us figure it out on our own. They confirm when we're in alignment and remind us when we've wandered out of it.

Building a relationship with your guides is incredibly rewarding—and it makes it easier to call on them when you have an established connection and find yourself suddenly "in the trenches." *A Course in Miracles* says, "If you knew who walks alongside you, fear would be impossible." For a time, I was afraid to call on my guides too often. I didn't want to ask for too much because I wanted them to be there if I *really* needed them. In reality, our guides never stop being on call, and they are on call because they want to be. Because they are not in a body, guides don't have egos, so you can't make them angry or annoy them. Truly, I promise, they want to help you whenever you ask, even if you ask multiple times a day.

Feeling unsupported or unguided can leave us stressed and feeling lonely or empty. If you've ever felt this disconnect, know that you have this support system available to you at all times. The mind might try to resist the idea that we're constantly being guided and supported, but the soul knows it to be true. Let it be your safety net. There is no shame in asking for help. The Universe will catch you when you fall.

Why Someone Might Choose a Difficult Life

What about the spirit guides of individuals who live in poverty or with severe illness? Where are they when their earthbound friends are in trouble? Choosing to come into a tough life situation is an incredibly selfless act, but it can be hard to view such circumstances in this way. Remember my friend, Matt, who transitioned at a young age after a car accident? I believe that was one of his teaching agreements (the details of which are not for me to know). He fulfilled the purpose he had set for himself and then departed. To choose a tough life or life experience is to be a guide and teacher for others. Perhaps, for example, a soul chooses to incarnate into a human being with mental illness. Obviously, this is incredibly difficult for the individual and their loved ones. Still, as the process unfolds, perhaps they teach their friends and family what it means to have patience and understanding, as well as how to love unconditionally. Life circumstances are not always about the individual experiencing them firsthand. Our human mind is self-centered by nature, so we automatically think every experience we have must be about us. But our soul is not this way at all—sometimes hardship is about teaching the people around us.

Experiencing a complicated life is not a punishment. Think about what you can gain (or have gained) from your challenging experiences. Can you use this knowledge for your own self-improvement? Can you use it to help others? View the situation from the perspective of the soul, not from the point of view that you have been a victim of circumstance. You have always been—and will always be—the driver of your destiny.

So, now that we know that logistically we're here of our own choice to expand and act as teachers, let's talk about how we can get the most out of our experience.

WHY YOU ARE REALLY HERE – PART II

Can We Have Fun, Already?

Our World Exists for Our Enjoyment

Now that you know why you're here, what's next? You're here, you're born, you grow … now what?

> *You are here to enjoy being a human as only a human can.*

Life on Earth isn't only meant for expansion—it is also meant to be filled with laughter, play, and fun. But by the nature of being human, we make it harder and more serious than it has to be. You are here to live out all of your wildest dreams and to have fun doing it! Anything is possible, nothing is off-limits. Believing this is not possible is just a limitation of the human mind and human culture. Miracles happen every day (as the laws of the Universe dictate). In the language of Universal energy, all things are possible, and as part of this energy, you are full of this infinite possibility. Trust that it is true and watch your world open.

One of my spiritual mentors, Robin Hallett, writes in her blog about an experience she had which demonstrates this concept beautifully. One night Robin awoke suddenly with the feeling that someone was in her house. After walking around and not finding a physical person or any disturbance, she sat down. All of a sudden, she heard a voice. A spirit had woken her up with an important message. Robin writes:

> *She spoke about something called Tangible Joy. This spirit was speaking excitedly about the irony of us trying to be so good while we're alive. Almost laughing, she talked about the way we're attempting to walk this pure and perfect path, one we believe will redeem us*

and keep us safe. One that makes us feel we are doing all the right things by renouncing what we actually LOVE about life. She was telling me it's this big cosmic joke: we spirits long to be in the physical to experience the tangible joys in life and then once we're human, we spend most of our lives in the pursuit of happiness which often means shunning fun. People do not understand, she said, once we croak, it's all different. And because we miss the most important parts, we are initially pissed when we return to the other side.

Let that sink in. If you transitioned out of your human body right now, would you have regrets? Perhaps there's another way to experience life. One that's aligned with our highest good and with what we came here to experience.

Every day we can choose the meaning of everything—we can make that conscious choice over and over again, every day and in every moment. The decision to have fun with our life comes from within. It's not a person, situation, or circumstance that makes you unhappy; it's your reaction to these things. You have control over your reactions. You get to choose where you align your energy.

Maybe that sounds easier said than done, but it doesn't mean that negative or uncomfortable emotions should be suppressed. On the contrary, acknowledging and processing our feelings prevents them from being buried inside of us. If we didn't do that, we would carry around those negative energies for as long as we kept them from surfacing. So, recognize the feelings, let them flow, and let them go.

The spiritual journey is called a practice for a reason. It's ongoing and never-ending. We are constantly presented with opportunities to exercise this practice. We can choose to see the world as loving and filled with kind people, or we can choose to see the world as unfair, cruel, and filled with untrustworthy people. What we choose to see is what we'll get. Our beliefs are reflected back to us in the world we see around us. *We create our reality.*

When you wake up tomorrow, ask yourself, *how do I want my day to go?* Despite what you might initially think, no one decides this except you. The weather doesn't determine your feelings, nor does your spouse, child, boss, or any other person or circumstance. You choose your perspective, always. So, give yourself permission to choose what you want! To decide that you don't have permission to have a good day because you woke up late or got stuck in traffic is to give up your power and hand it off to external factors. Rather, you could decide not to let other people or circumstances have influence over your experience. Initially, that might sound hard to do, but it doesn't have to be. Can you entertain the idea that it might be easy instead? We won't always decide on the positive side of things. That's natural and normal. There is always another opportunity to practice again.

You can take back your power. You can decide right now to align your energy to the frequency of love and joy. Finding small moments of alignment consistently adds up to big shifts in overall well-being. The consequence of living on autopilot and not enjoying the small moments is that life will pass you by without you even noticing. Pausing to devote just ten minutes a day to doing something enjoyable can be incredibly recentering.

This ten-minute practice will look different for everyone. It might be listening to a song that hypes you up. If you're like me, add dancing and singing (badly), going for a walk, or sipping a cup of tea. Ask yourself right now, *what can I do for a few minutes each day that I will truly enjoy?* Being consistent with this will disengage your autopilot (which is key to enjoying every day). When you go to bed and lay your head on the pillow, you can know that your day was in no way a waste because you prioritized *yourself*. This is part of living fully, with intensity and alignment. When you focus on what you enjoy, life becomes more vibrant. You'll dance through life instead of climbing uphill.

Living in alignment means being connected to the flow of natural abundance. Living in frustration or being upset means being out of alignment with our connection and can act as a reminder to gently guide us back into the flow. Sometimes, we feel we don't deserve to enjoy ourselves (which can be due to a multitude of reasons), and we punish ourselves unnecessarily (often, this happens subconsciously). There is no need to feel guilty about enjoying yourself and your life.

We don't need to earn enjoyment.

The phrase "work hard, play hard" is popular, unfortunately. It implies we must pay our dues in order to enjoy ourselves. In reality, we don't need justification. Play and fun are not just for kids, either! In general, adults take life too seriously. We forget how to play without worry, or how to play at all. Practice doing things (and not doing things) for the pure enjoyment of them and for no other reason.

When we are in a state of enjoyment, not only do we benefit from it, but it spreads and expands outward into the world. And, by the way, your state of enjoyment might look completely different than someone else's. We all experience enjoyment differently. For example, let's say two different people both get enjoyment out of watching a movie. One person may be laughing, crying, and talking throughout while the other is completely silent. That doesn't mean they both didn't receive an equal level of enjoyment from the same activity, just that it's experienced in different ways. One is not better or worse than the other. The way you experience enjoyment is perfect for you.

The more of us who enjoy ourselves here, the more good energy is brought into the world, and that can be felt by everyone on a grand scale. When your energetic vibration is one of love and joy, it will spread out and extend into other areas of your life—your home, your relationships, your work. The benefits multiply automatically.

Happiness and Where it Comes From

Society puts a lot of pressure on us to "find happiness" as if it's the only way we will live our lives "correctly." Everyone on social media looks happy all the time. Rationally, we know it's a highlight reel, but that doesn't seem to stop us from searching for it. The quest itself is what leads to a lot of *un*happiness. This can be particularly upsetting to people with anxiety, depression, and other states of mental or physical function where they inherently might struggle a bit more than others to simply "be happy." By nature of being an imperfect human being, a constant state of happiness is not sustainable. What we can sustain is our deep inner peace. Even when things get turbulent on the surface of life, we can return to the peaceful deep knowing of our truths to keep us grounded. We will have highs and lows; it's part of life. The constant is our soul, our connection to the Universe, and knowing we are inherently always free.

Happiness itself is not a life objective to be attained and maintained. It's a positive by-product of being in alignment with the Universe. When we are in alignment with the flow of the Universe, we naturally experience a level of joy because we are matching its higher energetic vibration. If we aren't in a state of constant bliss, then we might question our alignment. Alignment doesn't have to mean overt bliss or happiness. We can still be in alignment without laughing, smiling, dancing, or thinking, "I just feel so happy!" Alignment can also be a level of peace and contentment, relaxation, gentle wonder, or savoring and appreciating. When we remember who we are and why we're here, this comprehension comes with the relief of knowing that our mission is not the unattainable goal of chasing and keeping a certain high emotional state.

All that's to say, there's nothing wrong with happiness—the more people who are happier, the more good energy we have in the world. Happiness is an emotion that exists for us to experience, but it doesn't have to carry the pressure of being a daily life goal. We don't have to constantly beam in joy to be in the flow of the Universe and receive its goodness. What is attainable is a constant knowing that alignment is available to us at all times. It's never gone or forgotten from us, rather, we forget about it. Sometimes we just need to be reminded of its availability, and that we can always choose to align again.

We also tend to mistake happiness for something it is not. There's nothing wrong with being happy for the sake of having a good time (and the more often you do this, the better). The issues start when we think that acquiring things will bring us happiness or solve all our problems. I used to think that when I had a better job that paid me more money, finally, I would be happy. When I had a nicer car, finally, I would be happy. If I just had a beautiful home, a better body, a perfect relationship, finally, I would be happy. This is a sneaky trick the mind uses to keep us in a place of suffering. The mind likes to dangle the carrot right in front of us but always *just* out of reach. If we do manage to reach it, somehow, instantly, another one replaces it. It, too, is unreachable, and the chase—the wanting and the waiting—starts again. Falling into this mind-trap means there will always be something else we think we need to be happy. It's a vicious, never-ending cycle. We can never take in the present moment because we are always thinking about obtaining something in the future. Life is right now, and constant happiness is not an absolute requirement for experiencing a satisfying life.

If we're always waiting for something external to bring us happiness, we will never find it. This denial works the same for the past as it does for the future. If we believe that we can't or don't deserve to be happy because of an experience, a regret, or a loss then we are refusing to feel good now. It might sound cliché, but feeling fulfilled or joyful comes from within, and we can decide that we are worthy of experiencing it. It is not conditional on the past, future, or anything outside of us. Don't deny yourself the enjoyment of this moment because your past was better, or you think your future will be better. This moment, right now, is the only one that exists, and you deserve to have the best possible experience of it. Self-denial only keeps us in a cycle of excuses and certainly doesn't bring us closer to feeling better. We are here to experience the present moment, not to live in the space of delay. If we always live waiting for something to happen, we will never experience what we're waiting for. Should that thing or moment ever arrive, we won't know how to be present to enjoy it.

When we wait for the next thing we think will make us feel better, we tell ourselves that now is not good enough. Right now, *is* good enough. Enjoyment is hidden in the small moments of now, not tomorrow, and not by wanting or waiting for something we think will bring us happiness. We can experience freedom when we let go of the constant need for something more and our grip on the past. This is not to say we should throw our goals and dreams in the trash and settle for life the way it is. Not at all! If there is something you wish for, go for it! Reach for the stars, make a change, and align with the knowing that you can create whatever you desire.

It's great to have aspirations, dreams, and goals. We can find good feelings in the present and have an appreciation for our current situation while also co-creating a new reality with the Universe. When we vibrate in the peace of the present moment, we easily match the vibration of what we want. But we get the order of operations wrong. We think that achieving a goal or obtaining an item we desire will satisfy us, but it is just the opposite—our satisfaction brings these things toward us, effortlessly.

Sometimes, we find ourselves caught in conditionals such as, "I want to be happy, *but* I hate my job (therefore I cannot be happy)." Believing this is the same as saying, "I can't be happy because of something outside of me." Happiness is not conditional. Our enjoyment of life won't be determined by anything other than our choice to commit to it. That's it. We want to overcomplicate it because we're afraid to accept that we're in control of whether or not we have a joyful experience. Since many of us aren't enjoying ourselves, our first instinct is to put the blame outside of us. It's easier to believe that life is happening *to* us, that we are helpless victims at the mercy of outside circumstances. It takes brutal honesty to admit we're the ones in control; we're the sole reason for our enjoyment of life (or unenjoyment). The mind is always looking for excuses as to why we can't be joyful, but they're all defenses. It does take serious commitment to show up every day for ourselves and decide what we want. What if we decided that experiencing enjoyment could be effortless?

What is the quality, characteristic, or feeling of the person or thing you think will make you feel better than you do right now? That quality is what you seek—and it's inside of you already. You're looking for your own energy in the various forms you currently lack. In wanting a house, you might actually be wanting a sense of security within yourself. In wanting a partner, you might actually be wanting your own self-love. Think about what that might be for you. How can you cultivate those same qualities, characteristics, and feelings for yourself, now?

*

It might sound untrue, but some people are actually afraid of being happy, although this is usually a subconscious belief. When we live in an energy of fear, we automatically repel joy. Fear sends out the vibration of "I do not want this," so "this" will not come to you. Fear energy is a closed-off, non-receptive energy. So, why would anyone be afraid of happiness? This fear comes from the belief that when we are happy, it is always short-lived ... or something always goes wrong … or it was too good to be true. We would rather be unhappy all the time than experience the pain and disappointment of happiness ending. We may even repel happiness in the form of unconscious thought patterns we were taught at a young age. If our family was not happy, or we were told that "Only certain people deserve happiness," or "Life is hard," we might deeply believe that we are not worthy of happiness. We might be afraid of happiness because it is an unfamiliar feeling. Life as an unhappy person is at least predictable, and because it is familiar and predictable, it feels safe.

These limiting beliefs and others like them can be uncovered by asking, "If I were happy (or wealthy, or loved, etc.), what would my life look like?" Notice what images, thoughts, and feelings surface. Sometimes, thinking about a life that includes what we wish for seems so far-fetched that we cannot imagine it. It is too scary to think about, which is simply fear of the unknown. Or we fear something unpleasant may occur as a result of having what we desire. Questioning ourselves helps identify our fears around our beliefs. We can use this knowledge to see the differences between our life now, the life we desire, and the detrimental beliefs standing between them. Fortunately, thanks to the science of neuroplasticity, fears and stubborn thought patterns can be rewired into positive, productive beliefs. Current fears and limitations can be reframed and transformed into supportive beliefs instead (more on this in Chapter 7). No matter what keeps you from living your most aligned life (whether it's fear, feeling unworthy, or whatever), it can be changed.

Material Items

It's a common misconception that we must swear off all material possessions in order to be spiritual. As if earthly excess is impure and might blemish the spirit. This belief couldn't be further from the truth! While it is correct that the desire to have material items is an egoic one, that doesn't automatically make it bad or dishonest. There's nothing wrong with wanting to have a nice house, car, clothes, or whatever the desire is for you. Wanting these things doesn't mean you are a terrible person or that you have misplaced priorities. Who doesn't have material wants, anyway? We all do on some level, it's part of being a human with an ego. To denounce material things would be to denounce the physical world—the very thing we came to experience. We exist on this planet to enjoy its 3D gifts.

The misleading part of wanting material things is the unrealistic value and expectation we place on things external to us. We expect them to fulfill us; we think they will make us feel important and that others will respect us if we have them. Then, finally, we give ourselves permission to respect ourselves and be impressed by ourselves because of the things we have. The intention is misguided. It's fantastic to intend to acquire material things for their enjoyment, as long as we understand that they are temporary. However, acquiring material items with the hope of gaining respect, recognition, and fulfillment will only lead to disappointment. We need to keep the right perspective. We can choose at any time to grant ourselves the same permission, but without material justification. Our worth and value have nothing to do with our material titles or items. If we understand that the possession of material items isn't a source of purpose, and it won't make us whole in the long term, then we should feel free to embrace them to the fullest extent possible.

It will never be your purpose simply to amass wealth, cars, homes, titles, or accomplishments. Just as cooks add salt and spices to enhance the flavor in foods, material things can enhance your life. It's fun to enjoy these things, and we *should* enjoy them while also understanding their limitations.

Do you ever tend to keep certain things reserved for special occasions? I've bought many pieces of clothing that I liked so much, but I didn't end up wearing them for fear of wearing them out! They mostly stayed in my closet. But what's the point in that? If we can't enjoy the things we like on any given day, then why have them at all? Why is today any less or more special than tomorrow or any other day? Today you are alive—and that's worth celebrating. So, wear your favorite clothes for no reason, or drink a bottle of sparkling wine on a weekday!

We came here to enjoy the stuff of earthly life! We don't need to feel shame or guilt about taking pleasure in our possessions or enjoyable expenses. These things can *enrich* our life experiences. But they do not define it, they are not necessary, and they will not bring us long-term happiness, wholeness, or fulfillment.

Decorate Your Life and Your Space

Have you ever walked into a space that just felt good? How about a space that didn't? Energies are all around us, and we have the ability to create spaces that radiate energies that feel good. These spaces can positively impact the energy of the people who inhabit them. For most people, this primary space is our home. The individual expression of our spaces is different for each of us because they reflect our uniqueness.

Think back to your childhood or teenage bedroom. Hopefully, you had some (or a lot) of creative expression in making it your own with posters, art, or decorations, all of which you likely chose. As adults, we can still express ourselves creatively in this way, although we usually do it in a more refined manner. Take inventory. Ask yourself if your current surroundings reflect how you want to feel. If not, it might be time to make changes. This could be as simple as adding flowers, rearranging the existing furniture, or opening the windows to allow in the fresh air. Maybe it means getting rid of things that no longer feel aligned. Allow your intuition to guide you. Think of your home as a place dedicated to you and your joy. After all, it's a reflection of you. Match your vibration to your surroundings and your surroundings to your vibration. Don't be afraid to express yourself. Changing up your space changes the energy of the space! Changing the energy changes the result we get from experiencing it. Creating good feeling spaces for ourselves is a beautiful practice that can enormously impact our daily lives. Especially in today's world, where many of us spend all day at home. What does a space of good energy look and feel like for you?

Your Enjoyment is Paramount

Your own enjoyment is your highest priority (yes, *yours*, not others!). At first, that might seem selfish, but I am not suggesting that we don't care at all about others. We simply cannot pour from an empty cup. Putting ourselves first allows us to fulfill our own needs, which then allows us to have the capacity to share our light with others.

Do not compromise on making your own enjoyment and self-care a priority.

So how can we cultivate more enjoyment for ourselves? One way is to shift our perspective to one of awe, appreciation, and excitement. Viewing every day with curiosity, gratitude, and wonder is a great practice to support long-term life satisfaction. Constantly adopting a fresh perspective allows us to discover and savor experiences that previously may not have gotten our attention. It can open up our world—suddenly, hidden viewpoints and feelings are visible and available. When we slow down to explore and discover what's here to enjoy, life can be fascinating. Try slowing down enough to notice birds, flowers, people's smiles, the breeze in the air;

anything, and everything possible! Pause for a second. Take it in. We take so much of our beautiful world for granted by letting it pass right by us.

Have you ever noticed that when talking to a young child, we exaggerate our speech? We say things such as, "*Wow!*" and "*So great!*" to demonstrate for them our excitement, joy, and wonder. Sadly, at some point, we stop being curious about our wondrous world. As adults, we get used to things. They stop having a "Wow" factor for us. The marvel can get lost if we let it. Yet, there are amazing things happening around us all the time. This magic deserves our attention.

Seeing anew means seeing the light in all people and all things. Noticing the little things has a way of shattering daily monotony and cultivating a sense of appreciation for the vibrancy of life. We can wake up from a robotic state of living by returning to this practice constantly. For example, try talking to yourself for a day in the way you might speak to a small child (self-talk in your head is okay!). Narrate your day in your head with curiosity and excitement, as if you were seeing everything for the first time, and it was all an exciting adventure. I know that might sound ridiculous, and you might feel silly. But it's not as far-fetched as it might seem. If you've ever visited a beautiful place, seen a gorgeous sunset, or eaten an incredible meal, you probably did this exact thing as you were present for the moment with awe, joy, or appreciation. This practice is a beautiful way of bringing an air of thrill, possibility, and joy to seemingly mundane things. Don't just look, but really stop and *see.* Don't just touch, but really stop and *sense*. Don't just taste, but really stop and *savor*. It is possible to find wonder in the ordinary.

We can also reframe our thoughts (in the childlike voice or not) to change how we view something. For example, instead of saying, "I have to work out today," replace that with, "I *get* to work out today" or "I *want* to work out today." This is everything! Remember, you don't *have to* do anything. You are free, and you always have a choice. You *get* to do things, and only if you want to. When I rephrase the "have to" statements in my life, I remember that I'm the one in control. We can see things other than as chores or obligations; we do them because we choose to, not because we are forcing ourselves to. Letting anything become a "should do," "have to," or "need to" invites in an energy of pressure, guilt, and negativity—instant joy zappers.

Sometimes we desire an outcome, but not the process. Frankly, I don't get excited about doing laundry, but

I do appreciate and enjoy having all of my clothes clean. "I have to do laundry" can be changed to "I enjoy clean clothes," and that tiny shift in the perception of the task at hand makes all the difference.

We can also gain a new perspective on things we might already find enjoyable and make them even better. When I'm enjoying my workout, for example, sometimes I think, *how lucky am I to be experiencing this feeling of strength? We don't get to do this in spirit form!* This perspective is just as applicable for big moments, too. We can enjoy vacationing, for example, and take in a new or different scenery, cuisine, and culture. It's fantastic. When you focus on the potential enjoyment of our world, life seems more like a privilege and fun adventure.

For me, this new perspective is a far cry from my "I didn't ask to be born!" moments. It makes me want to gather up all the earthly experiences I can. This is my only chance in this lifetime to do so. When I go back to the spirit world, and my co-spirits ask me about my trip, I can tell them about all the amazing earthly things I got to experience.

My dad often says that the meal he's eating on any given day is the best one he's ever had—which is often met with rolling eyes. "How could that be true?" I'd say. "When you just said that yesterday. And the day before that." Finally, though, I realized what he was doing was a genius way of living life. Why can't this meal in front of you right now be the best meal ever? The meal you are eating is the only one that exists because the present moment is all that ever exists. There's no reason we can't glamorize every meal, every drive, every coffee, and really—every moment.

Seeing and holding on to the beauty in everything, even if only for a few seconds, can be life changing. So, whenever possible, find awe. Feel its excitement. Appreciate. Be curious in every moment. Life is so much sweeter when we slow down enough to capture these moments.

The Universe is alive in everything. Can you see the beauty in everything, even the boring or bad? Being mindful in this way is how we can cherish everything and waste nothing. Too often we deem the trivial things unimportant or become disgusted by what we might deem "bad," but little things can be magical, and "bad" can be viewed with gentle curiosity and compassion.

Indulging, savoring, and experiencing every moment as one worth living is the practice of a lifetime. It took me many years to realize that life is not handed to you; instead, life is what you create, what you make of it, and how you experience it. It's in your control, and it's your choice. What can you do today to celebrate, just for fun (it doesn't have to be something big)? How can you carve out moments to savor?

What If I Don't Have Time to Prioritize Myself?

Putting yourself first is about living life on your own terms, contenting yourself first and foremost. Yes, most of us lead busy lives with packed schedules, but thinking there is no time for ourselves, and our enjoyment, is an excuse, an illusionary story created by the mind. In dating, when someone is interested in us, they *will* make time for us, regardless of how busy they are. Well, it's time to start being interested in yourself, my friend! Who and what are you placing as a higher priority than yourself? We can't devote ourselves to those people or things if we have not fulfilled our own needs and wants first. Try releasing the "I have no time" narrative and replacing it with one such as "I can find time every day for myself, no matter what." You might have to get creative. Shift things around—create space. You will know how to find it if you let your intuition guide you. When we put ourselves first, we don't just honor our human selves but our souls too. Your soul is craving acknowledgment and a chance to shine, so please don't shut it out. Self-care is not selfish; it's an act of love. If taking one hour to nap or do absolutely nothing in the middle of the day is what you need, you are not lazy. That may sound like a luxury to many, but it's a more extreme example on purpose. We tend to throttle our needs and wants versus intuitively listening and honoring what our soul is telling us. You are your number one priority. Start honoring the fact that you're a magnificent piece of the Universe, and you deserve to be regarded as this magnificence!

Reality Check, Every Day Is Not Always Good

We all have bad days, bad weeks, bad months, even bad years. It's not realistic to expect that we will feel good every single day, although that's a great intention to have. It's not rational to have "Good Vibes Only." Bad things happen. We are human and imperfect by nature, and there will be times where something sets us off or goes wrong, and we are not in a headspace to even think about our joy. *It happens,* and when it does we don't need to beat ourselves up about it or shun or suppress any emotions we might have towards it. We try so hard to push away bad feelings, especially when we've experienced feeling great. Of course, we don't want to feel bad when we know how good it can feel to feel good. We automatically think we must have done something wrong by attracting a negative situation to us or that it's a step backward in our progress. Our mind tries to guilt-trip us and analyze what's gone wrong. No one is positive enough all the time to have energy that repels every bad situation. It's not grounded to think we will never experience another unpleasant day.

So, what do we do when things go sideways? Well, recognizing it is a great first step. There have been times when I've gone down a negative spiral and didn't even realize I'd done it. So, if you can recognize how you feel, you can offer yourself compassion. Our instinct might be to try to force our way out of our emotional dilemma, but what we resist persists, the opposite of the result we want. We can be so quick to judge ourselves, our feelings, and our responses to them. We don't need to feel guilty for feeling negative emotions or having negative thoughts. This puts unnecessary pressure on us and makes us feel like we've done something wrong. It happens to all of us. We can begin to move through it by allowing ourselves to feel whatever it is that's bothersome. Often, giving these feelings and emotions center stage allows them to bow out and move on. Sometimes it takes more time, and that's okay too. If we are gentle with ourselves during the process, we won't stay there forever.

A rough patch is temporary—it will pass. Try not to judge it. There might even be something you can gain from the experience, whether you realize that now or not.

THE AMNESIA, FALLIBILITY, AND FRAGILITY OF IT ALL

Am I Dreaming?

(Not) Remembering What You Signed Up For

Waking up to who you are and why you're here can be, well, scary. It might feel as if everything you've known before was a lie. It might feel confusing—because now, you don't know what to think. But taking time to turn inward and reflect is imperative in the process of awakening. It's okay if it feels worse before it feels better. There is light at the end of the tunnel. In the awakened state lies understanding and freedom.

To be awake is to recall the truth. This is the "big remembering." It's easier to believe the truths about who we are and why we're here when things are good, but not so easy when things are tough. But the truth is always there, whether you ignore it or not. The more you can practice remembering the truth, the easier time you'll have navigating difficult situations.

Have you ever gone to the grocery store with only a mental list in your head? I do this all the time. If I only need about five things, I convince myself I'll be able to recall them all. Once I get there, however, suddenly I can't remember what I came for. I'll usually remember three items or so, but then I think, *I know I came here for something else, what was it?* I just can't put my finger on it. Coming to Earth is a lot like being in the grocery store and forgetting what you came for. Suddenly, we're in a new environment surrounded by thousands of distractions, and we can't recall our list (our truths). We wander through the aisles, hoping that something will trigger our memory. We do our best, and then we leave. Back at home, everything is clear again, the amnesia is gone; we remember our list.

The same is true for us. We wander through life, hoping we'll be reminded of our truths (either consciously or unconsciously). We hope to have "lightbulb moments" about our deeper connection to something greater than ourselves and where we fit in. Then, when we transition back to spirit, we find clarity again. We know who we are, why we went to Earth, and we see the big picture from the perspective of our souls. But, of course, at that point it's irrelevant for living our current life. We need to remember *now*. So, I'm here to hand you your grocery list. I'm here to remind you what you have forgotten. Because if you don't have all your ingredients, you can't make the recipe. If you don't remember your truths, you can't live your most fulfilling, abundant life.

Come with me for a moment. Let's imagine we are traveling back to the spirit world, your true home. Here you exist as your energetic self. Here you'll find family and friends who have transitioned, and you'll meet your spirit guides. Your guides are energetic beings who have agreed to assist you as you live out your human experience. They try to keep you on your outlined path, and they help you any time you need them. At some point, spirit guides have also lived as human beings on Earth, so they know what it's like and are well-prepared to help.

Imagine for a moment that a soul is "conversing" with its guides, and that this is the soul's first time coming to Earth. I imagine the conversation before the first incarnation to Earth goes something like this:

Spirit ready to incarnate: "I think I'd like to experience being a human being and go to Earth."

Spirit Guide: "Thanks for expressing interest in Earth; let's make it happen. Life on Earth means you will experience incredible things. You'll live in a physical body which will be able to touch, taste, and hold tangible items. You'll be able to experience emotions because you will have a brain and a heart. You'll see breathtakingly beautiful sights with your eyes. Overall, it's truly a fantastic experience."

Spirit ready to incarnate: "Wonderful! I'm so ready; when can I go?"

Spirit Guide: "Well, first we need to decide together what your life plan will be. This means selecting what you would like to teach while you are there. It also includes choosing who your family will be and the other means by which you will draw to you the necessary experiences that will allow you to act as a teacher. Oh, and you should know that anything can happen once you enter into this agreement. Human error is abundant on Earth.

> We will do everything we can to keep you on track with your plan, but ultimately you will have free will to do whatever you want. Would you still like to go?"

Spirit ready to incarnate: "Yes! I believe it will still be very much worth it! I can't wait to taste Spam!"

> **Spirit Guide:** "You're going to love it. One last thing, you must agree not to remember that you came from here or who you've been before...."

Okay, that last part trips me up too because I do not like Spam. I'm just kidding (not about the Spam, though, sorry if you like it). We have to agree to a certain amount of amnesia, or all sorts of weird things might happen.

Past Lives and Why We Don't Remember

Many people know about and have even "seen" their past lives (often through past life regression hypnosis). If we are supposed to have amnesia, why are we able to access past life memories through hypnosis? The people who seek out past-life regressions are ready for the information. They can handle it. Otherwise, the events that lead to them having a regression would not occur. Humankind as a whole is probably not ready to embrace this "woo-woo" concept, hence a level of secrecy around past lives exists (to some degree). As we grow collectively, we will all be able to access our souls' truth and our past lives more readily. We are not there yet, so our past lives stay hidden, except to those who actively seek them out.

Yet, other individuals (often children) have reported remembering who they were in a past life without any hypnosis at all. They've recalled in detail the names of people, places, dates, and events they could not have otherwise known. Some of their memories have been verified, and it's probably more common than we think. For now, we can see it as further confirmation of our deeper consciousness.

In general, it's safe to say most of us don't remember who we used to be. For many of us, past life memories are a total blackout. For others, some prior life recalls might come through in the form of flash memories, déjà vu experiences, or dreams. If you pay close attention, you might start to recognize them. But we come to Earth willingly, knowing what the trip entails. It includes that we must agree, voluntarily, to forget. If we didn't, inevitably, there would be huge problems.

Aside from humanity's unpreparedness, there are good reasons for why we don't remember, such as:

1. Comparison
2. Lack of importance
3. Respect and appreciation
4. Complications

Comparison

Imagine for a moment that you're a famous actor or actress. Fast forward to your next life, where you chose to incarnate into someone who works a regular 9:00 a.m. to 5:00 p.m. office job, or you chose to be someone in a tough life situation. Do you think your next life would go well if you were able to remember that you used to be famous and had a glamorous life with anything you wanted at your fingertips? Not only would that be difficult (because you'd be making constant comparisons between your current and past life circumstances), but you wouldn't be able to focus on the life you were in. The present moment would be overlooked. The comparison would cloud the experience you were supposed to have as someone different, with different things to teach.

Lack of Importance

We don't remember who we were in our past lives because, frankly, it's just not that important to know. There is a difference between remembering your existence as a soul and remembering your specific past lives. The first one is important, the second one is not. Prior incarnations are an experience of your soul, not of your physical body or mind. The soul transcends time and experiences different lives and bodies, and the soul remembers. So, it is only essential that you recognize the eternalness of your soul, that your human birth in this incarnation was not "the real start" for your soul, and that the transition you will make at the end of this incarnation is not "the real end." The other lives you've lived don't have an impact on who you are right now. Your current experience is *supposed to be* your only focus. As long as you understand who you are right now, all the other bodies and worlds you've inhabited don't matter.

Respect and Appreciation

I always thought if we could remember our past lives, we'd be better off because we could avoid certain pitfalls we may have encountered in the past and utilize our memories of prior experiences to help us in our current life. But it's crucial that we start with a clean slate because the life you're in now must be treated with care and respect. For example, say you knew who you had been in the past, and you know who you will be in the future. Would you write off this life as worthless if you decided that you didn't like this body and this life? "Who cares if I'm an average person now?" you might say. "I've been a queen in the past, and I will be a celebrity in the future. Therefore, I'm just going to put my head down and ride this one out." Or worse, "I'm going to end this life prematurely." See the problem here?

By deeming this current life "too boring," "too hard," or "terrible and worthless," its purpose gets disregarded. Every life has meaning and purpose, and it's not a mistake. As we know, every life experience is chosen carefully by the soul itself. Deciding to dismiss it means you would not enjoy your life to the fullest extent your soul intended, and the teachings you wanted to teach would remain unfulfilled.

It's important to understand and appreciate your present experience. The only way to ensure this is to remove the opportunity to judge your current experience against a former or future experience by forgetting.

Complications

Not only would lack of appreciation and different life comparisons be harmful to your current experience but there could also be crossover repercussions and complications. Currently, not everyone accepts the idea of reincarnation. We are all on our own paths, and the diversity of those paths is beautiful.

Imagine for a moment a (fictitious) person named John. A psychic told John's uncle (let's call him Frank) that John had been his father in a past life. John had wronged Frank severely in that life. Armed with this new information, Frank confronts John, explaining what he has learned, and demanding John apologize. As you might imagine, John is shocked, confused, and hurt. With zero knowledge of his own past lives (and not knowing whether this information is accurate), Uncle Frank has eroded his and John's relationship in the current life with only a few sentences. At best, their relationship will be forever changed, at worst, it will be forever damaged. This is a good example of the kind of complication that might ensue if we could remember our past lives. People would seek an apology, even revenge, and view others as someone that person currently is not. Can you imagine if someone began bragging about how they used to be royalty in another time? That would likely be met with strange looks from anyone unaware or closed off to spirituality or reincarnation. At this point in time, a world like this would be confusing, even dangerous.

If we want to know about our past lives, we must separate this knowledge from our current life. In the story above, our fictitious Uncle Frank clearly did not have the sensibility or spiritual maturity to handle the information the psychic gave him. What we learn, in this lifetime at least, we can never unlearn. We are all not operating from the same belief system. Because of that, the amnesia puts us on a somewhat level playing field.

Warning, Please Do Not Try This at Home.

Earth life comes with a disclaimer. With all the good things that come with being a human, not-so-good things exist as well. It's part of the human experience. Phrases like "we're only human" and "human error" imply that being human comes with a certain degree of fault: *We are not perfect.* We are briefed on the nature of free will before we come here. Earth is an "enter at your own risk" planet.

That being said, our time here is temporary compared with the immortality of the soul. Human life is fragile and short. We've all heard about treating each day as if it were our last. There's a lot to gain from heeding this expression. We don't know how and when we will transition back to being only our soul selves. But we do know that we came here on purpose, for an experience, to help up-level humanity, and with an understanding of the possibility of error and challenges in life.

Free Will vs. Destiny

The concepts of free will and destiny can be difficult to grasp. At first glance, the idea of our souls having free will on Earth might seem like a paradox. How can we have a soul plan yet also have free will? Destiny and free will cooperate with each other. While you come here with a plan, how you go about it and what you choose to do with it is your choice.

Destiny is aligning with your highest good and what your soul outlined as its mission. Free will, on the other hand, is being more aligned to your human self.

Part of the experience of being a human is the joy of having free will. A reference for my fellow millennials:

It's like being a Sim that's been left in free play (try to remember to feed yourself and not burn the house down). Free will has to exist on Earth because, by design, humans are imperfect. Without free will, we would be helpless puppets at the mercy of a preordained fate. That would be no fun, and our existence would essentially be pointless for us.

Since you do have free will, everyone around you has free will too—which leads to an infinite number of possibilities and combinations of actions. We are presented with opportunities to make choices constantly. The big things in our lives are part of our soul plan. Our situations, the people in our lives, and our challenges are all on purpose, and there is something to gain in every challenge we experience.

When we are facing a challenge, we feel uncomfortable. This uncomfortableness is a call to action. If we know that our discomfort is alerting us that it's time to get back into alignment, we'll handle these on-purpose challenges more easily. Our more minor decisions, on the other hand, are usually left to free will. Decisions such as "What outfit will I wear today?" or "What movie should I watch?" are free will decisions. That doesn't mean that our small decisions can't play a part in our larger soul-design. What seems like a small decision might lead to something larger or down a new path, but in general, we make plenty of inconsequential choices.

The Universe wants you to take action in the face of adversity. We are supposed to be active creators of our life experience. If we were not meant to be effective participants, there would be no free will. We are in control. When we find ourselves at a crossroads, needing to make a decision, sometimes we worry about making the wrong choice. However, there is no such thing as a wrong choice because any choice we make is right. Each choice may lead us down a different path, but that's the beauty of free will. Ultimately, we end up at the same destination if the outcome is something we are supposed to experience. Perhaps choice "A" leads down a path with less resistance than choice "B" may have had. Choice B may be more challenging, but in that case, you have simply presented yourself with an opportunity to expand because there is something for you to gain from it. In this way, the choice you make is always the correct one. It's a choose-your-adventure world.

The next time you find yourself worrying or stressing over a decision, know that whatever you choose is the right choice, and it will lead you to where you're meant to be. It's a matter of whether there is something more for you to gain in this area or not. You are always exactly where you're meant to be. We can rest assured in this because what is meant for you will always find its way to you, and what is not meant for you will steer clear of you.

The fact that you came here on purpose means that you *must* be an active participant. You weren't promised perfection, and sometimes being a human being is just plain hard. But you *were promised* free will in your thoughts and actions. There are certain non-negotiables when it comes to life plans and experiences, but your free will determines how, when, and where you will go through them. You get to choose. To "choose your destiny" might sound like an oxymoron, but it's about learning to continuously listen to your higher self. Your higher self will always lead you into alignment with your destiny.

There is always an opportunity for growth. The one who goes down with the ship will be taught again.

—The Guides, through Paul Selig

WHAT YOUR PURPOSE REALLY IS

What Am I Here to Do?

The Big Mix-Up

For the longest time, I felt like I was doing life wrong. I was suffering from burnout because I was doing the same boring routine every day. I was exhausted. I had no purpose and no direction. But an inner voice kept whispering to me that I was supposed to be doing something greater. I had a *knowing*: *I was here for a reason*. The problem was, I had no clue what the reason was. I thought I just needed to find the right career and the right relationship; that once I had checked all the boxes on the list of what society said I should do, I'd feel purposeful, and all my problems would be solved. After all, our whole society (more or less) is following this same life strategy—how could it be wrong?

Spoiler Alert. The relationship and the job I had were not my purpose. Sure, I checked all the boxes, but I was not fulfilled in the way I expected to be. My inner knowing that I was here to be something greater was persistent—and it got louder as time passed. By the time I turned thirty, I felt that time was running out. *Surely*, I thought, *if I don't know my purpose by now, I'm doomed to never find it.* This infuriated me. I wrote in my journal, yelling at the Universe, "I would have never agreed to a life where I didn't know my purpose by now! This is BS!" I was wasting my life with every passing day and not knowing what to do about it, just that I should do *something*.

If you've felt this persistent, annoying feeling, you are not alone. It's your soul trying to get your attention. It wants to be recognized; it wants to express itself. You haven't failed, and you're not too late. You're right on time, exactly where you're supposed to be.

We all want to know our purpose. We want to feel like we matter and that we add value to this world. Yet so many of us don't know our purpose—we're unhappier than ever, more disconnected than ever. We're told that advancements in technology are supposed to make our lives better and easier (nothing against technology, by the way). Still, the desire to live a meaningful life doesn't get easier. Instead, it seems to move farther and farther out of reach. The good news is this recognition for wanting something more can be a great catalyst for change.

You do have a purpose. It lives within you, and no quest or pilgrimage is required. Having a purpose is just the desire to share, serve, and help other human beings. Society tells us that "having a purpose" means being successful. When we feel purposeless, we look outside of ourselves for validation. We hope our social media, qualifications, or job title will make us feel significant and purposeful. Usually, though, this fulfillment is short-lived. We can get so caught up in chasing likes, followers, wealth, degrees, and accomplishments that we miss what's right in front of us. We have unrealistic expectations, and ultimately, we're discouraged—and we're back at it again, searching for a purpose.

Purpose is simple. The quicker we realize this, the quicker we will leave the grand illusion of perpetual disappointment. Purpose is who you are when you're expressing yourself as your best self. Purpose is not just for you but also for others because there is a component of service to purpose. Your purpose is to recognize your true nature—that you are a soul in a body and an extension of universal energy—and to live from that place in everything you do. Your individual and unique expression fulfills your purpose.

Kindness is part of your purpose.
Love is part of your purpose.
Shining at your brightest possible wattage is part of your purpose.
Teaching others is part of your purpose.

Your purpose in this lifetime is to recognize that you have the light of the Universe within you and to shine this light in all you do—and as only you can. This is the gift you can give to the world. Your gifts are acts of service, and service is part of your purpose. The inner knowing to shine will light the path to your unique purpose.

I had always expected a representative from the Universe to appear one day out of thin air, to tell me that I was born to be a chef, an astronaut, or a painter. I waited years for that *Aha!* moment in which the

Universe would spell out what I should be doing. I was jealous of people who instinctively *knew* their purpose in life. It took me a long time to realize that it hardly ever works like that. Some of us can indeed tune in to the guidance of our higher selves better than others. Hopefully, you won't spend as many years as I did waiting, wondering, and being frustrated. For the Universe to tell us that we're supposed to have a specific profession would be far too restrictive. The Universe doesn't see us compartmentalized and organized into categories of occupations. We do that ourselves, and we do it because we are the ones to figure out how we can best serve.

Purpose is showing kindness, love, and expressing yourself in ways that bring you joy. If this feels disappointing, try to keep an open mind, just for now. I certainly felt that way—I was upset that it wasn't grand or definable in one word. You are not forgotten—you do have purpose. You are unique, with a special energetic fingerprint to mark in this world.

The light inside of you wants to be bright. It's in your nature, just like the stars—(and you are star stuff!) you are cosmically designed to shine brightly. You've chosen to be here at this specific time, so own it. Rise up and step into your destiny. The world needs your light. It is not the time to be dim—it is the time to turn up your luminosity to its full wattage.

Stop acting so small. You are the Universe in ecstatic motion.

—Rumi

Your Sacred Shine - From Dull to Sparkle

As an au pair in Berlin, one of my tasks was to help polish the silverware when guests were coming over. I would put on the white polishing gloves and rub away the tarnish on what seemed like hundreds of forks, knives, and spoons. It was a tedious, time-consuming task that I can't say I enjoyed. Humor me for a moment—picture yourself as one of these forks, spoons, or knives. You are covered with tarnish (just in need of a freshen-up). I'm going to polish you and make you shine by removing all your uncertainty and fear. Now you're shiny and ready to serve!

So why don't we shine willingly most of the time? How do we get tarnished? By living our lives on autopilot. By living without purposeful direction. By living without joy and appreciation. If our tarnish is unchecked for too long, it builds up. This can make it difficult to remember that we're actually shiny by nature. The quickest way back to shining is to remember who you are because the soul itself cannot become tarnished.

*

When I was a child, I was always told to be on my best behavior and never to make anyone go out of their way for me. My mind interpreted this as needing to stay small, undetectable, and perfect. As a result, for most of my life, I've attempted to stay as invisible as possible. I dimmed my light in order to feel safe. I convinced myself I could survive without anyone's approval because that would mean "being seen."

Have you ever felt that you needed to dim your light? Perhaps someone else made you feel that your thoughts or opinions were unimportant, that you should "tone it down" or make yourself small. Perhaps the fear of others' judgment kept you from shining. Shrinking ourselves and our light is a defense mechanism we use to get by undetected. If you can relate to this, allow yourself a moment of compassion. You did what you needed to do to survive, and no guilt need be attached to it.

Deep down, we want to matter. Deep down, we want to shine. You are meant to shine your light—and when you shine brightly, you show others they can shine brightly too. I encourage you to be big and bold and to take up space unapologetically.

In addition to having a spectacular experience, you are here to express your authentic self. How that manifests is up to you. Harness your power—own your talents, strengths, and uniqueness so you can shine and be of service to others. Can you see that expressing yourself as you is synonymous with purpose? View yourself as unlimited. Move beyond any restriction your mind might try to place on you. See the possibilities as endless—they are yours for the taking! If something lights you up, it's for a reason. It can be effortless to shine if you believe you can.

Your soul already knows how it wishes to shine. Your challenge is to listen closely, hear its whispers, and act. Of course, this is a work in progress, an ever-evolving, lifelong journey. As your interests and priorities change over time, your purpose may shift and change as you grow and expand. You may have multiple purposes. Perhaps for part of your life, you will be passionate about business and find purpose by serving as an entrepreneur—and in another part of your life, you will be passionate about photography and find purpose by serving through capturing images. Finding your purpose is about discovering the things you care about and putting that care to use for the highest good of all. As long as you are shining, you are living your purpose.

Like a lot of people, I struggled to discover the ways in which I like to shine. Something always felt like it was missing. In 2019, I took a stand. I decided to complement my unfulfilling full-time job with a purpose-driven, part-time job. Because I enjoyed fitness and wanted to help others get healthier, I decided to become a part-time personal trainer and group fitness instructor. Pretty quickly, I realized that I wasn't enjoying either one. This realization was devastating. I was hoping that one of these jobs would be "it," that they would be my purpose and also my ticket out of the corporate world.

It's disheartening to be let down on the quest to find purpose. My past "failures" held me back; I was scared to fail again. That's what my ego would have me believe, anyway. Failure isn't pleasant. But truthfully, there is no such thing as failure. Really, these were opportunities for growth. Today, I look at these experiences as little mini explorations that were actually a necessary part of my journey. Trying on these different roles gave me a range of experiences while also teaching me things. So, they were not a waste of time. For example, while working as an au pair, I learned valuable communication skills. As a group fitness instructor, I was working on overcoming my fear of being seen. All of your experiences have served you, even if you don't yet understand in what ways—perhaps you learned a skill, or you learned what you didn't want. Even if you can't see it now, it was all intentional and for your highest good. You are only defeated if you decide that you are.

Joy and Listening to the Whispers

Eventually, I decided to forget about receiving a "silver purpose platter" from the Universe, and I began to prioritize joy instead. What harm could there be in trying a different approach? So, I substituted finding my purpose with experiencing joy. I found that being more intentional about my enjoyment of life made me care less about finding my purpose. In fact, I kind of forgot about it. Being in alignment with joy allowed me the clarity I needed to hear direction from my soul. All of a sudden, the words for this book started to burst forth. Sharing this information with you lights me up and makes me feel fulfilled and purposeful.

Will it be my only purpose? I don't think so. But being in alignment allowed me to hear the guidance that was waiting for me—and this book is the result.

Follow nudges from your soul, even when your mind tells you they don't make sense (or that they are dumb). Follow what you are drawn to, even if you don't know why. A tiny bit of purpose is sprinkled into everything you do. Follow the breadcrumbs. We never know where they may lead.

Don't worry about whether your exploration will end up being a serious passion for you or whether you can make money at it. Instead, focus on the pure enjoyment of it. Start small. Make little moments of enjoyment of utmost importance. Small moments of peace and joy, small moments of service, small smiles, and connections—they all add up. Doing something enjoyable every day will help you unfold your purpose. The more you do this, the more nudges you will get from the Universe. Pay attention to signs and synchronicities. You are getting guidance all the time! Pay attention to your dreams, to things that catch your eye—when you scroll through social media, when you hear lyrics and melodies on the radio, when you see repeating numbers on the clock such as 11:11. When something makes you stop and look, it's intentional. Perhaps you hear the perfect song lyric at the time you most need to hear it, or 777 is part of the license plate number on the car in front of you in traffic, reminding you that miracles are abundant. Sure, you could brush these off as coincidences or as insignificant. Choosing to be open to receiving is half of the conversation with your guides. If you see patterns repeating, pay attention. All of these things are messages from your spirit guides, and they are helping to steer you in the right direction.

When you live from a place of truth and knowing, you will receive guidance. If you get a clue, follow it! Don't let your ego tell you it doesn't make sense. Do things for pure enjoyment. After all, what is the point of reaching your so-called destination if you haven't enjoyed the journey? If you do that, when you get there, you won't know how to appreciate it.

Want to know if you're doing the right thing? Ask yourself: "Does it inspire me?" "Does it bring me joy?" "Does it intrigue me or pique my curiosity?" Don't know what you like? That's okay. I didn't like anything for years. I was too tarnished. Many of us wouldn't know what to do for fun if we did have extra time because we're busy living on autopilot, with our minds focused on the past or future and completing our daily to-do lists. But this is the problem, isn't it? We are conditioned to prioritize working and accomplishing over self-care and fun. We chase productivity and neglect and deny our wants. Before we know it, they become buried.

So, what can you do to get back on track? Imagine you don't have a job or any obligations. You can spend your days doing whatever you want, without limitations. What would you do? The critical ego might start to tell you all the can-nots or impossibilities, don't let it. It might take some time to get an answer, and that's okay. Once you've got it, explore how you can incorporate your answer into your current life on a smaller scale. If you'd spend your days singing, for example, then maybe this means taking just five minutes in your day and make it your fun time to sing your heart out. Maybe it means joining a choir or signing up for singing lessons. There's always a creative way to get us closer to what our soul calls for.

From time to time, I like to revisit this question. It's a good way to check in and see if what I want is what I'm actually living. Growing up, I wanted to be a ballerina, and for a time, this was my answer to what I'd spend my days doing if I could. I had taken ballet classes when I was younger, but I felt too old to return to them. Still, there had to be something I could do to bring me closer to this dream. Then it dawned on me, *why not try a barre class?* I fell in love with the workout and decided I liked it even better than ballet. This one decision is what led me to become an instructor for a time. Not only did I find something that was exciting to me, but I also faced my fear of being seen head-on—something I wouldn't have otherwise done voluntarily. This was a valuable growth opportunity that led me to the next step in my journey.

See how this works? Following an inclination or trying something new opens up a whole world you may never have known existed. You never know where something might lead. I once brushed off things that I now enjoy. "Meditation? I tried it, didn't work for me." "Painting? I'm no good at it." "Reiki? Sounds weird, no thanks." Now, these are all things I love to do. So, why did I have that experience initially? Because I was getting in my own way! My resistance and unwillingness to try were blocking me. I was misaligned. My vibration was too low to care or see another way. Things will start to shift when we can move from a lower energy to a higher one.

Living in a low vibrational energy is kind of like living in a fog. You can't see what's in front of you, and you can't see anything ahead of you. It seems like you're trapped in hopelessness, with no way out. As you raise your vibration, however, little by little, the fog dissipates. Things come into focus; things seem possible. When you live at a high vibration, not only does the fog disappear, the sun shines. Doing things you enjoy allows the Universe to flow through you, and the more you allow this, the closer you come to living your purpose. The more time you spend doing things you enjoy, the more you are in the flow. The more you are in the flow, the more you are open to hearing the Universe.

So, pay attention. Take inspired action—even if your ego says not to. (Tell your ego to take a nap and try it anyway.) If something is inspiring or intriguing, it's on purpose. Your likes, dislikes, interests, dreams, and desires are yours for a reason—they belong to you. Your soul carefully chooses the things that light you up. It's the soul's way of leaving markers for your human self. They were designed to keep you on your destined path. Your soul knows you will ignore what doesn't excite you and follow what does. It's all cosmically designed.

When you do things that light you up, you feel aligned, and things flow in the right direction. When you feel down, it's no coincidence that everything seems to go wrong. We panic. We think, "Oh no, I've gotten myself into this situation, and I can't get out." We feel guilt and shame.

It's true that we are responsible for where we are, but we don't need to beat ourselves up over it. That only increases the density of our cloud. Pause, take ownership, forgive yourself. It's okay. You got here because you didn't know any better (or you did, but you didn't care enough to change it). Here's how to get back on track:

- Be kind and gentle with yourself. No blaming, shaming, or guilting towards you or anyone else. Regardless of where you're at, all is well. It's not a race to get out of the fog. It probably took some time to get into this cloud, and it's okay if it takes time to clear it out too.
- The key to clearing is feeling. Prioritize things that make you feel good—whatever that looks like for you. Do this, and over time you will be guided to better-feeling things. Keep riding these feelings up and out.

There's no need to keep looking at and pushing for the "end game" of finding your purpose. I pushed for so long, trying to reach an unattainable place, and I got nowhere (except into a state of anxiety). Go back to basics: find inspiration, curiosity, enjoyment, and get into the flow of it. "Living in the flow" means living as a conduit for the loving energy of the Universe and letting bad situations pass right through you without resistance. Letting love flow through nourishes you in the process, and things fall into place effortlessly.

Answering the call of purpose is about enjoying every little step of the way. It's not an instant transformation, which is why it's important to pay attention to the nudges from your soul and the Universe. Over time, those nudges push you to your perfect path, even if it doesn't seem like it at the time. Taking even a slight interest in something is not pure coincidence. It's part of your purpose. It may be a small stepping stone or a large one—it's not important to know which it is. What's important is that you take action. Your mind will try to label and analyze every part and piece, but don't worry about that. It just wants to be in control because it can't see the big picture and therefore can't make sense of it. It's actually a good thing that it doesn't make sense to your logical mind. That's one way you can tell it's divine guidance because if you could rationalize it, then it might be your ego's desire instead. The soul doesn't need it to make sense to you; it speaks in feelings, not thoughts. A series of intuitive nudges that don't make sense might seem erratic, but they all purposefully contain your energy. They are therefore cohesive on a grand scale.

How to find and follow your purpose path:

- Know that your purpose is already within you, that your soul knows how to reveal it to you in perfect timing. All you have to do is be open and willing to listen.
- Prioritize enjoyment by doing things that bring you joy, regardless of how silly your mind thinks it is.
- Pay attention to the whispers from the Universe, ignoring whether or not they make sense.

Enjoy this process without having a goal in mind or needing to control it. There are thousands of small steps on this journey and being present for each one is part of the whole point.

It's not an overnight process; it's not meant to be. We live in a world of instant gratification. We want instant solutions to our problems. We don't want things to take time; we don't want to trust in unknowns. Part of the process is showing up over and over again in different ways. Everyone's journey is unique, and there are an infinite number of paths to take. Try to enjoy it by continuing to put one foot in front of the other and believing that the Universe is leading the way.

Your Light Is Valuable

A common misconception is to think that if we have a purpose, we have value and that if we don't have a purpose, we don't have value. Part of the reason the search for purpose drives us so crazy is because we're trying to prove our value in the world. But we don't need to prove anything to anyone, and we already have intrinsic purpose and value. The Universe doesn't hold contests—the sun, the rain, and the mountains don't have to prove their worth. They just *are*. Value and worthiness are abstract ideas made up by human beings to make some people seem more or less important than others. Simply by existing, you have worth. Worthiness does not *happen*; it just *is*. You are not here by accident; therefore, you have value. You don't need to change, prove yourself, convince anyone, or do anything to be worthy. Allow yourself to accept your worthiness and value fully. What you accomplish and what your qualifications are do not equal your value or worth.

Your value is not your name, age, place of residence, degree, certification, job title, or accomplishments.
Your value is not your house, car, or the money in your bank account.
Your value is not your number of followers on social media, your number of friends, or your relationships.
Your value is not determined by anyone or anything else.

These items are distractions that pull you away from this truth. The truth is that your value simply just *is*. Some people use these things to justify their value because they cannot accept that value is intrinsic. These things do not matter. You are a teacher. You are kindness. You are love. There is nothing more you need to do. You are, always have been, and always will be valuable and worthy.

Teaching as Purpose

If you're unsure of your unique purpose, you can still start living other parts of your purpose now. Showing kindness, love, compassion, gratitude, and gentleness are ways you can express your purpose immediately. For example, when you hold the door for another person or give someone a smile or genuine compliment, you are sharing your light. Practice kindness toward others and yourself. Every one of your actions demonstrates your light as a teacher.

What does teaching look like, exactly? It can take many forms. Aside from what we think of as traditional educational instruction, teaching is happening around us constantly. Each one of us is a teacher, and we are always teaching through living demonstration. Every time you interact with another person, you are teaching through your words and behaviors. You teach through the way you interact on social media. You teach through the way you interact in everyday situations. Sharing your unique journey as a teacher for others is purposeful action.

With each human body comes a new opportunity to teach something—or many things. When you expand and grow, you share with others by living through your light and teaching by example. This is powerful. Don't underestimate your light. Wherever you go, so does your light. There is a never-ending reserve of love within you. Be the example of this loving light. Be an example of love, kindness, and compassion. Be an example of freedom and joy. This is how you teach and reach.

The Trust Fall

Possibly the hardest part of viewing purpose as kindness, love, and shining your light is having faith that this is the truth and having patience and trusting in the process and the timing of the Universe. We all want a romanticized version of purpose, but I'm here to break it to you: It doesn't usually happen like that in real life. It can be a hard pill to swallow, I know. Set aside the quest for purpose and reorient to finding enjoyment. When you're in the realm of joy, thanks to the law of attraction, you will start to attract more joy, abundance, and all things amazing. Surrender your expected outcome. Don't analyze it—just let it be, and let it be easy.

You are amazing. You matter in this world. To quote *A Course in Miracles* again, "I am the light of the world. That is my only function. That is why I am here." You are where you are supposed to be, exactly who you are supposed to be, in the exact timing it's supposed to be happening in. You don't need to be in a hurry or feel like you're missing out on anything. Your seat is reserved just for you.

What you seek is seeking you.

—Rumi

Don't worry about the how's. Don't let anxiety get the best of you, thinking of all the ways things could play out. Give yourself permission not to worry about not having the answers or not being able to see every step of the way forward. The more you relax, the more you open the door to let in whatever it is you are calling to you. Your openness to receiving and believing that anything is possible will be reflected back to you in the form of your life. Let go. Let the Universe take care of the details.

WHY WE SUFFER

Sometimes We Struggle Unnecessarily

This Is Not a Test

In the spiritual community, it's common to hear the term "Earth school," the idea that we come here to learn and master certain lessons. Personally, I find the term "Earth school" depressing, which may be partly because I did not have an enjoyable experience at school. Many people loved school and have fond memories of it. For those people, the concept of Earth school may resonate in a positive way. There is nothing wrong with the term—it's just a label, after all. What resonates for one person may not resonate for another, and we are all free to interpret our existence in the way we want to.

That said, I don't think Earth is a school. This notion has never sat well with me. In my view, we are not students, nor are we here to prove we can pass some strange test distributed by the Universe. It's difficult (for me) to imagine an existence based on learning specific lessons and overcoming certain trials or believing that over enough lifetimes, if we learn our lessons, eventually we will become fully evolved souls (kind of like a graduation).

It is true that the idea of "lessons" offers a convenient explanation as to why we go through hardships in life. We want to know there's a reason we're experiencing difficulty, that it's not all for nothing, and that it's not random. But it makes life as a human being sound like a punishment and a test. I don't know about you, but *I do not* want to chalk my whole existence up to a test! If we are from and of the Universal Energy, which is pure conscious love, would the Universe have set this up to punish or test us? It's an absurd concept and contrary to the energy of love and joy. The Universe is not cruel—it wants us to feel loved, to be love, to share love, and to have joy. Period.

I don't believe we are here simply to learn lessons. While learning is a part of our experience, in my view, it's secondary to being a teacher and enjoying the human experience. This life is not a punishment, as soul-lesson-learning might suggest. Perhaps, over several lifetimes, you might select the same teaching themes in different ways, but *you choose*. You are not forced or punished, and you cannot fail. It is possible for an incarnating soul to repeat life topics voluntarily, and the reason behind that is a secret of the soul. But as we teach each other in different ways, we increase our capacity for love. We level up and expand our collective consciousness. We are always teaching each other. So, why then do we suffer?

Less Is More

As we already discussed in Chapter 3, we're also here for the enjoyment of our world—which is the opposite of suffering (duh). The journey of life as a human being was never meant to be some kind of unpleasant trial. As a society, we have this idea that in order to come out on the other side as a better, more enlightened person or someone who has achieved great success, sacrifice and suffering are required. We put ourselves through so much suffering with the goal of avoiding suffering! This is just not needed.

Many people believe there are rewards for putting yourself through pain and struggle that are, frankly, unnecessary. These "rewards" are usually monetary or in the form of achievements, and the only way to get them is through hardship of some kind. It's a human construct. Just as a representative of the Universe is not going to appear out of thin air and hand you a silver platter with your purpose engraved on it, they are also not going to appear with a gold certificate rewarding you for your self-induced struggle. As I said, this life is not a test to be passed.

We make ourselves feel unworthy, we compare ourselves to others and judge ourselves harshly; we put ourselves through unnecessary pain. We are not here to be punished. So, why do so many of us feel that we need to suffer? It's because we've decided that pain equals success and achievement. Suffering feels safe to many because it is familiar. We know it so well that it can be confused as being a natural state. But at any moment (how about now?), you can decide to stop the madness of suffering by deciding to no longer align with it.

Without challenge, suffering, or sacrifices, we might feel like life would be too good to be true. When things are going great, do you feel like you're waiting for the other shoe to drop? We expect our luck to run out at some point! If we aren't careful and don't recognize that this belief is actually a lie, this can become a self-fulfilling prophecy. Right there, whether you realize it or not, you've invited in resistance to goodness. This is a collective, limiting belief that lots of us subscribe to. It's not true.

Suppose that none of us ever knew suffering, and existence on Earth was a blissful utopia. Without the reference point of some challenges and upsets, we would have no genuine appreciation for joy because it would be all that we knew. We wouldn't have the capacity to savor it or feel gratitude for it because we wouldn't have experienced a range of different emotions.

This idea that suffering is required comes, in part, from individuals our society considers successful. Pause and think of the most successful person you know. Why do you think they're successful? Is it because of their net worth, recognition, or achievements? (Let me just say that you should not compare another person's life to your own, nor should it be a factor in how you judge whether what you're doing is good for you.) These "successful" individuals will often speak of all the sacrifices and hardships they went through to get where they are.

Simply put, our society values and respects suffering! How messed up is that? We think we'll earn the respect of others through suffering and sacrifice. Society values what and how much you produce, how much you accomplish, and how fast or early in life you can produce and accomplish those things. It all leads us to feel like we have to be "on" and "doing" all the time. There's so much pressure to do-do-do, so we are not left behind and so that others do not perceive us as lazy or less-than.

Think about how backward this whole concept is. We expect life to be hard. We believe that success is unachievable without major sacrifice. It's no wonder we set ourselves up for struggle—this is the "normal" framework society shows us. But it doesn't have to be this way! Suffering does not equal success, and success does not mean we have to be stressed, busy, or productive. What if we decided it didn't have to be hard? What if we invited in another idea of success, one that cultivates an energy of ease and possibility? It's not about how fast or early in life you produce or achieve. What if real success was daily enjoyment and alignment? What if real success was living life on your own terms?

From an early age, we try to prove ourselves constantly. First, this "proof" usually comes in the form of retaining knowledge and information. We are taught language and are asked to repeat it to prove that we know it. It continues from there in more complexity as education progresses. If (for whatever reason) we stumble, we start to think that we are not intelligent—and this is reinforced in the form of bad grades or disappointment from our parents or peers—and then we accept it as truth. We devalue ourselves and experience guilt or shame, all based on generic standards. We learn early in life to associate not achieving with punishment, and that idea, unfortunately, follows us into adulthood. It's no wonder we confuse worth with knowledge and success with productivity. But news flash, the information stored in your mind does not equal your worth, and achievements do not equal success.

Similarly, how busy you are does not equate with your worthiness. Many people believe that they thrive on chaos and complication. Why? Because without chaos, they are bored, and they have no choice but to take a truthful look at their lives. Many people are afraid of their own shadow and will do anything to avoid it, often by staying occupied. You might hear people say, or say yourself, "I'm so busy," or "I'm so tired." We stay overly busy to the point of exhaustion to avoid taking an honest look at the role we play in our unhappiness. We want to avoid facing the truth: only you are responsible for your state of being. The only one punishing you is you. There is always another choice. We could decide not to align to the twisted goals of our society and decide instead to live our lives in alignment with our highest good.

This doesn't mean that we must shut off the outside world or pretend that bad things don't happen, that we live in a state of blissful unawareness, or that we should ignore or suppress our feelings about the things happening outside. Rather, we can stay grounded in the reality of our world, and at the same time, decide to put our energy elsewhere. Your energy is your currency. Where would you rather spend it, on disaster or goodness? We can acknowledge current events and have feelings about them while still choosing how to respond. With each event, this process becomes easier and quicker. In between the action and response lies a space. In that space, you get to decide—where do you want to align yourself and your energy?

I'd rather flow through a difficult situation than fight it, kicking, screaming, and complaining the whole way. I've tried that, many times, with little success. When swimming in the ocean, you never fight against a wave—if you do, the wave will tire you out and overtake you. The same is true in life. Always flow with it, never against it. Spiritual teacher Eckhart Tolle says we should view every situation as if we have chosen it. That's not being ignorant or giving up—it just makes every experience easier. Does staying in the energy of suffering serve you in a positive way? Certainly not. Suffering brings more suffering. So, this is a gentle reminder to move with the natural flow of the Universe. Be in alignment with the path of least resistance.

You have personal responsibility for your own life. You get to make choices. When I was a barre instructor, I would offer options and modifications for moves in my classes. "Remember," I told my clients, "You always have a choice!" I saw my clients struggle through moves I demonstrated but not making any modifications. They didn't want to believe they had a choice, that there was more than one way to do it right. They would instead do the original version with worse form than the modified version with better form and efficacy. There is always another option, and part of choice is deciding you have a choice!

If you feel you don't have a choice, ask yourself, honestly, "Am I stuck in victimhood?" It's easier to blame others and the world for our circumstances than it is to take an honest look at the choices we've made (and continue to make every day, at every moment). Are you contributing to your own suffering? Or are you contributing to your own joy? For example, you decide what and how much media and other people's thoughts you consume. You decide what you think and what you say. You decide the significance of situations. You decide your response to all of it. Don't sit by idly in pain and suffering. You are in control of your life. You can break free from suffering and step into feeling better. The more you choose love and joy, the less you will choose suffering. With practice, choosing joy will become more and more natural for you. (Just like choosing to suffer felt natural for so long.) Let your mind work for your highest good in this way.

We Still Get to Grow

Let's face it, life on Earth can be exhausting. It might feel like the world is designed to make you fail and that traps are set everywhere for you to fall into. It can feel like this, but it's not true. See adversity as an opportunity to awaken. See disappointment as a redirection to a better way. Adversity and disappointment are just the Universe's way of saving you from spending time on things that aren't meant for you. It's a beautiful design, but we aren't always able to see that in the moment. No human being is perfect. Therefore, we have opportunities to grow and improve. Growth is part of the spiritual journey. Hopefully, you will be able to look back on the challenges you've gone through and see how you grew from them.

*

Just because we are not here to prove we can pass a test on certain lessons doesn't mean we don't ever learn or grow. We do. In fact, learning and growing are hugely important parts of our human experience. Growth is often a product of challenge. We have free will, and therefore error. It's just the way our world is. Imperfection breeds opportunities for challenges to emerge. Challenges are part of your life plan (as discussed previously). Life presents us with opportunities for growth all the time, and some (if not all) of these opportunities are on purpose. When an issue, challenge, decision, trauma, etc., comes up for you, it's revealing itself on purpose so that it can be confronted and healed. This is no accident. Growth requires confronting it. It could be something small (such as forgiving your partner for forgetting to pick up dinner on the way home) or something big (such as dealing with childhood trauma). We don't grow easily when we are comfortable. Why would we? When we are comfortable, there is nothing forcing us to adapt in some way.

You see, growth is a critical process for bettering ourselves and the world. Feeling stuck, stagnant, bored, or unhappy means, you have expanded up to the boundary of where comfort meets discomfort—and it's time to push past that boundary. You've outgrown your space, and you're ready for a bigger one. Viewed in this way, growth is exciting!

It doesn't have to be seen as negative, even though it might be uncomfortable. Challenge can be a good thing. Stressors can cultivate inspiration and adaptation, and bad situations can lead to great things. They can push you forward when you might otherwise have stagnated where you are. If you chose the international experience (you did, since you're here on Earth), you are already stepping out of your comfort zone. This requires vulnerability, which is where growth happens. Sometimes there's unavoidable (temporary) discomfort, which feels unfamiliar and unsafe. But if you see your challenges as opportunities for expansion, and you remain open to learning and growing every day, you will expand.

Uncomfortable experiences get our attention. When we notice them, we can step back and ask ourselves, "What can I gain from this? How can I grow from this?" To not learn and grow would be to never evolve or advance, either individually or collectively. Learning and growing are like repotting a plant. There comes a time when it needs more space because it has expanded and has even more expansion to do. When you learn and grow, you are plucked from your comfortable, familiar pot and put into a newer, bigger pot. You can see it as scary and align with the fear of change, or you can see the possibility and align with the wonder of it. Your roots can grow and expand until you're ready for yet another, bigger pot. The alternative to repotting is stunted growth and shallow existence. Don't choose to stunt your growth because you are afraid of the unfamiliar pot! Even enlightened people have opportunities to grow. There is no finish line for expansion as long as you are a living, breathing human. Every challenge, every person, and every opportunity can be your teacher if you choose to welcome it in this way.

*

We incarnate on Earth with the full awareness that our admission price is experiencing some level of struggle. It's okay—it's part of the experience. We come to feel joy, of course—as much as possible—but we also come to experience the entire range of feelings and emotions (which includes sadness, anger, fear, to name a few). It's an experiment in learning how to regulate ourselves. Once we gain a feeling for what these different emotions are like, we understand where we want to spend more time—and where we don't.

Karma

Karma is a word everyone is familiar with. In the context of spirituality, it serves as a popular explanation for the unpleasant parts of life. But I don't believe our souls are here to pay off karmic debts from other lifetimes. Again, that would make life a form of punishment and imply that judgment exists in the spirit world—where there is only love. I do think karma exists on the earthly plane in the form of energetic vibrational frequency, however. For example, if you cut rudely in front of someone in line at the store, you send out a vibration of negativity and greed. You will attract the same negativity to yourself because of the law of attraction (which says your thoughts and feelings act as magnets). The opposite is also true. If you "pay it forward" in the Starbucks drive-through and pay for the order behind you, you send out a vibration of positivity and abundance. You will therefore attract more abundance to yourself. Karma is essentially the law of attraction in action on the earthly plane. Your every action sends out a vibration that you will attract back to you. This happens whether or not you are consciously aware of the choices you make. You are held accountable for your choices by the law of attraction, regardless. Becoming aware allows you to use this to your advantage. When you choose to send out a positive vibration, not only will you attract it back, but you also contribute to the positive energy in the world. You can increase the light in the world through small (and big) acts. Never forget that your light and your choices are powerful. I don't want you to worry whether you will have to fear a debt repayment in a future life or that you are living one now. Instead, focus on whether your words and actions now add more kindness to the world.

In other words, I don't believe that karma transcends lifetimes. This life is not a punishment or a reward for a former one. Karma is limited to this lifetime and is determined by your thoughts and behaviors. Negativity attracts negativity, and positivity attracts positivity. It's your choice. The former is living from the mind. The latter is living from the soul. Anger, fear, jealousy, disgust, sadness, upset, defensiveness—all are examples of negativity that will move you farther from your soul connection. Love, compassion, forgiveness, kindness, gratitude, wonder, and excitement are all examples of positivity that strengthen your soul connection. Energetically speaking, every action has an equal reaction. Everything—every thought, every action, everything you do—carries energy. So, you are choosing with the energy you put out at all times. With it, you are choosing your future. You are creating your life.

You Are Not a Victim

The world we live in has formed us all, and the shape our lives take depends on our experiences thus far. If we feel lost as adults, we might blame the generation before us for the way we were raised and for the world we've inherited. This blame is a pointless endeavor. Those who came before us didn't know any better, so they couldn't do any better. They were in the same position we are (just a generation earlier, having been raised by the generation before them who also didn't know any better). It's cyclical. When generational traumas aren't recognized, they don't get healed. You are not a victim of circumstance. You can break this cycle. You can wake up and say, "Hey, there's a better way, and I am the change."

When you decide to stop being a victim to circumstance, you stop holding someone else responsible for your problems. To live as a victim is to let other people sit in the driver's seat of your life and to identify as a helpless passenger. To clearly see the role you have been playing brings healing; it frees both you and the people and situations you have held responsible for your problems. You can bring about the shift to heal your own life, and you can stop negative patterns from repeating. How? Recognize with compassion that it's not your fault—it's nobody's fault. There's no one to blame, and you are not a victim because you can be free. Blaming gets you nowhere; it will only keep you stuck. It will not heal you. But forgiveness and release will move you forward. The past cannot be changed; it unfolded the way it did for a reason, and the future is in your hands. We can forgive all those who came before us. Holding on to resentment, anger, or pain will keep you in a low vibration. To be free and at peace, you have to let it go lovingly. I promise you; it's not serving you to hold on to it.

You do not need to be a prisoner of a job title, a diagnosis, a condition, an idea, etc. At any moment, you can decide to release it, to no longer identify with it. This is not the same as dismissing something or ignoring it, however. For example, I have had eczema since I was two years old. It is a diagnosis I have had for as long as I can remember. All I have ever known is a body with itchy skin. I don't ignore it (that would be nearly impossible!) or claim it to be unreal. It's real, and it's good at getting my attention. But I don't let it *define* me. I see it as a signaling system. I know that if it's bad, then I must be stressed. It reminds me to slow down. I choose to see it in this way versus seeing it as my enemy. I am not its prisoner.

Slow Down, Let It Go

Both society and our minds tell us we should always be busy, that we should be doing more. We put unnecessary pressure on ourselves to go, go, go constantly. This is a recipe for burnout. When we push ourselves, we think others will see us as strong, but actually, we are strong when we honor ourselves and our needs.

It is often said that we are human beings, not human doings, which means practicing more of just *being* versus *going* and *doing* constantly. Sit quietly, without technological devices distracting you. Sit alone in a quiet space and reconnect with your highest self. Learn how to be with yourself. Learn how to be in the present moment. Do nothing, and just *be*. Stillness is a necessary part of the healing journey. There is freedom in this practice because when you sit in silence with your thoughts, you remember who you are and why you're here. We run from and are distracted by our thoughts as if we're afraid of our true selves.

Perhaps you are now realizing you could slow down a bit more. When you can recognize this for yourself and take appropriate action, you will experience relief. Hurrying will not bring harmony but simply haste. Can you set aside the idea of always trying to achieve? Everything you think you need to do will still be there waiting for you if you feel you want to pick it up later.

When we slow down, we might feel unsafe. But it is safe to relax. It's an act of self-love that will bring more peace to your life, and there is no rush to get anywhere or do anything. You create every sense of urgency, and you can un-create it. You are always right on time.

Release and surrender are powerful tools we can use to create space for receiving good—and there is so much good in the world to see and receive. Remember, you're not alone in this journey. Use this to your advantage. At any point, you can hand it over to the Universe. Whether you have a problem or a question, the Universe and your guides are always there to help. Sometimes I forget this and find myself pushing for an outcome, trying to control the whole situation. I plan carefully, overthink, and get stressed.

While I was living in my previous apartment, I disliked it. My husband and I were both working from home in a couple hundred square feet. My ego liked to constantly remind me of all the reasons why it was so unpleasant. I was hyper-aware and downright obsessing about it. My negative focus made me feel *terrible*, and I was tired of my resistance toward it. It was exhausting to be upset all the time. I wanted a way out, so again I asked the Universe to help me change my perspective. I was fearful because if I surrendered my problem, I no longer had control over the outcome. I wanted it to turn out a certain way, but my way wasn't working. I decided to trust in the divine plan instead of my own. I vowed I would stop trying to force a change, I would stop complaining, and I would forget about the whole thing until the lease was up. I decided to prioritize enjoyment instead. *I can find joy here and now, regardless of where I live,* I told myself, because that joy could come from many sources that had nothing to do with what I disliked. Once I stopped fixating on it, I became free of the resistance I was attaching myself to.

The same process can be used for overcoming fear. We can offer our fears to the Universe and ask for them to be transformed into love. We can do this in different ways, and you will know which one feels right for you. It might be through prayer, meditation, visualization, or writing in a journal—or perhaps using a combination of these. My preferred method is visualization. In my mind's eye, I see my spirit guides standing in front of me. Then I see myself literally handing whatever is bothering me over to them. If it's something intangible like a feeling, I will give it a physical quality so that I can hand it over. I end the visualization by thanking them for their help and guidance. This technique has worked for me many times with great success.

If you are serious about letting go (and that means letting go of outcomes), surrender. Surrender doesn't mean sitting back with your arms crossed and expecting the world to unfold in front of you. Action is good; the Universe encourages action. The difference between surrendering and controlling action is that in the latter we attempt to dominate the situation and its outcome, which ends up increasing the resistance to our desired result. In the former, we are not attached to an outcome because we are secure in the knowing that everything happens in divine timing—we know that what is meant to be will be and what is not meant to be will not be.

You might initially feel resistance to releasing and surrendering. This is a completely normal reaction. It takes practice and patience. When you've learned to let go of fear, it becomes easier and easier each time. Each challenge you face, big or small, will expose another angle of fear. That fear can be disguised in many forms, such as jealously, sadness, or anger. Whatever form it takes, it's always another opportunity not to be sucked into it. Living without fear is living without expectation. It's giving without the expectation of receiving. It's loving without expecting reciprocation. It's exploration and adventure without expecting failure or success. It's having fun without reason. It's teaching without expecting credit or recognition. This is how you can greatly diminish disappointment and sadness. This is where freedom lies.

Releasing your grip on fear is freedom. The more you squeeze something you're afraid of losing, the more it slips through your fingers. Not only that, grasping blocks you from receiving because nothing can enter a closed-off state. To release is an act of courage. It might be scary, but a release is freeing. Allowing space for the problem, person, or situation (or whatever it is) to air out and breathe creates room for the organic movement of the thing you were chaining yourself to. If it's meant for you, it will stay. If it's not meant for you, let it go in love. Trust that it's supposed to be this way. Whether you like it or not, whether you ride it or fight it, notice it, or ignore it, the wheel of life keeps turning. Everything is impermanent. You don't want anything sticking around that is not meant for you.

There's no need to grip ANYTHING.

Not even your spouse or your home, not anything or anyone, because it's all temporary. Your time here is temporary. You or someone you love is not guaranteed another day here. Your house could burn down tomorrow. While this might sound negative, it's just a reminder of the fragility of life, whether that's literal human life or the life of material things. When we surrender and trust in the Universe, we can find peace. Letting go is the ultimate freedom. It will allow you to see that you don't need to do anything or change anything. Everything is as it is. Surrender is an amazing, powerful practice. It's to remember that we don't have to be strong all the time or fumble our way through the dark. Life can be so much easier by way of asking for help. Whenever possible, surrender. Author, speaker, and spiritual teacher Gabrielle Bernstein has a saying that I love and remind myself of often, "When you think you've surrendered, surrender more." Actual freedom is not attached to anything—not the past, the future, any outcome, or any person, place, or thing.

How can we suffer less and still meet our challenges and grow? Surrender. This may seem like a contradiction, but it is not—you do not have to suffer. When you hit an obstacle in the road of life, remember, your choices are:

1. Step into the pain of it, be stuck to it, be helpless, and hope to be rescued from the situation, or
2. Don't resist it and see it as a chance to grow, knowing you can hand this problem over to the Universe and choose your response to it.

The Power of Thoughts

Often, we suffer at the mercy of our own minds. Thoughts can have all the power or none at all. The difference is whether or not you believe in a thought. If you do, you give it power. If you don't, and you let it flow through you, it has no power. When I was a kid, somehow, I knew about the power of manifestation and being in alignment. When I was falling asleep, I used to imagine things that I wanted and *feel* the excitement of them, as if they were already mine. I knew instinctively that this was a powerful practice that could turn thoughts into reality. Of course, I did not know how it worked. Sometime after childhood, however, I forgot this practice, and I didn't remember it until I watched the documentary, *The Secret*, which put an explanation to practice. The secret is the power of alignment. When you are in alignment, things fall into place effortlessly.

I have used this practice time and time again—to manifest small things and big things. I have manifested cars, apartments, jobs, and my husband (just to name a few). There was intention and feeling behind these desires. But when you are in alignment, you also manifest bonuses that you didn't intentionally ask for. That might be a free coffee, a front row parking spot, or a kind compliment from a stranger. It's like having the best luck all the time. The trick is not to let your ego talk you out of it. Don't let it say, "This is too good to be true! Surely, your luck is about to run out!" That would be a lie, and too often, we let the ego convince us that such lies are true, which then is reflected back into our reality like a mirror. Modern physics agrees that everything, at the most sub-atomic level, is energy. When we see things from an energetic viewpoint, we see that there is enough good energy to supply us for a lifetime—it can't run out or be too good to be true because it is infinite. The ego doesn't understand energy, but the soul does.

You can take control of your life and watch it change into everything you ever wanted. Nothing is impossible, *nothing*. Stay open to the possibility that whatever you want might not come or manifest in the way you expected. The Universe is clever. We always think we know best, but we don't. Why? Because we can't see the big picture. We must be patient and trust that these things can take time and will appear in their own unique and surprising ways. Just because something doesn't happen immediately doesn't mean it isn't going to happen—it might even happen in a way that is even more magical than you could fathom.

This has happened to me more than once. Going back to my apartment story... I wanted to move more than anything. I was trying to control the situation before I handed it over to the care of the Universe. Around this time, another apartment in our building became available. It was bigger and had more natural light, which I wanted. However, my husband did not want to sign the lease on it, and since we could not agree, we decided not to take it. I was upset. I was mad at the Universe. How could it betray me like this? The timing seemed perfect; I couldn't understand why it wasn't happening. Looking back, I could not see that something better was already in the works. I suspect we might have stayed there if we had taken that apartment because we wouldn't have wanted to move again. We might have liked it and felt comfortable there. This would have closed the door on what *did* happen (which was a bigger and better move than I had expected). Not only did we end up moving to a bigger and better space to suit our needs, but we also moved out of state, which was a big dream of mine. I'm not sure it would have happened if we'd settled for the other apartment. Let this be a reminder to trust in the process of divine timing. It's more than possible for doors to appear where before there was only a brick wall. What looks like a "no" from the Universe may actually be a "No, because there is something better."

Life's a Beach

The expression has a lot of truth to it. Metaphorically, it reinforces the idea that we're here to enjoy our world, but also the world may as well be one big sandy beach. By putting your hands into the sand and manipulating it, you can create anything you like, from a small, simple sandcastle to a large, intricate one. Your thoughts, feelings, and intentions are like the water. Add them to sand, and you create something that sticks together so you can create shapes and forms. You're here to create the sand sculptures of your dreams. Together, we shape our world through our beliefs and collective sculpture. What seems to be a rigid physical world is actually quite malleable. We just have to recognize this. Changing what it looks like starts with you, in your area of the beach. When you sculpt the life of your dreams, it shows everyone else what we are all capable of creating.

We can get so caught up in our desired outcomes we forget that the artistic process is a creative one to be enjoyed. The actual process of sculpting and creating is meant to be savored just as much as the finished piece. We are never really finished anyway. We are constantly creating and sculpting until we leave this Earth, so we might as well aim to enjoy the process. What do you want the next chapter of your life to look like? You are the one that gets to sculpt it in the sand!

YOUR EGO AND MOVING FROM FEAR TO LOVE

Befriending the Frenemy Within

The Ego Isn't Going Anywhere

For a long time, my ego was way out of balance. It was out of control; it ran my life, and I didn't realize it. I'd constructed a six-inch-thick-concrete ego to mask the hollowness, loneliness, and sadness I felt inside. Nothing could get through because it was in full protection mode. While living in Berlin and working as an au pair, I got the wake-up call I needed.

Once a week, my host mom, her two pre-teen girls, and I would take a yoga class. Each week I would lay out my yoga mat and sit down and wait for the instructor to begin. It never crossed my mind that I should help lay out their mats too. I grew up in a largely do-it-yourself household, and it made sense to me that everyone should be responsible for their own mat. Of course, I was responsible for the children, but it didn't connect for me that they might need help or that it would be the polite thing to do. Looking back, I'm ashamed of my egoic tunnel vision, but it was all I knew. After months of this, the mother of the family I was working for confronted me. "You are so self-centered," she said. She told me I was not good at anticipating the needs of other people. I couldn't believe what I was hearing. I would never have been rude or unaccommodating on purpose, ever. I simply had not been able to see another way. This was a wake-up call. Her words stung. I sat with them. *Were they true?* I asked myself. My behavior was largely unconscious, and I wasn't aware of it until this confrontation. This was the beginning of the end for my dominating ego.

What is the ego anyway? Scientifically speaking, the ego is the part of our mind that understands us, the world, and everything in it. The function of the ego is to help us be aware of ourselves and our surroundings.

It tries to keep us safe, often in a detrimental way, through negative thoughts. It creates a sense of self-importance so that we can feel significant in the world. Do you know that negative voice in your head, your inner opponent? That's the ego at work. When we think of someone with a big ego, we often picture an overconfident or arrogant person. When the ego projects itself outward in those forms, it's acting from a place of protection. Having an ego comes with the territory of having a human brain. We all have one. The ego is a necessary part of who we are, and it's not going anywhere. If we can learn to peacefully coexist with it, it can work in our favor instead of against us.

In the spiritual space, there's a concept called "ego death," the idea that in order to be enlightened or to embody as our highest self, we need to overcome our ego (kill it, essentially). If you are seeking true enlightenment in the Buddhist sense, you may be interested in pursuing "ego death" (although it can never truly die as long as you are living), but I'm suggesting you don't go to such extremes. The ego gets a seriously bad rap, and understandably so, but it is something we can learn to tame rather than kill altogether.

So, what's so bad about the ego? The ego thinks it's vital for us to take everything personally, see everything as being about us, and see everything as an attack or threat to our well-being. It judges, assesses, and overanalyzes. It loves to make up stories and tell us that we have all the evidence in the world to support our negative thoughts and feelings. It's always on the lookout for such evidence, and it stockpiles it for later use.

Quite simply, your ego does not want you to be truly happy—ever. If you were, it would lose its control over you. It hopes that you quest endlessly but never find what you are seeking—or, if you do find it, that it's temporary, and then you'll be back where you started. Your ego is like the one person around a campfire who's telling scary stories nobody wants to hear. When it gets going, it can be hard to stop. The narratives the ego throws at you can be pretty crazy, even downright wild and unrealistic. It can spin you so deep down into a spiral of anxiety and fear that you can no longer see what's true.

I think we can all relate to the doom-and-gloom voice in our head—the negative one that tells us why and how everything can go wrong, or why we shouldn't, can't, or won't. The stories it tells us can range from simple doubt to extreme and elaborate tales of fear and anxiety.

Negativity can be engrossing and addictive. Some people believe that they thrive in emotions of anger, upset, and sadness. It's almost like a high. I'll admit, sometimes it just feels good to complain. The ego loves it. Complaining and putting our attention on the negative makes us feel better—temporarily. But it doesn't serve us in the long run or solve any problems. Complaining, judging, and ego stories are like quicksand; it's easy to get trapped in them. The issue is that we use these things as excuses not to shine and pursue our dreams and passions. This can create serious mental blockages, which keep us from living a fulfilling life. Now, all of that might sound like good reasons to want to rid ourselves of this thing but hear me out.

Believe it or not, the ego has positive elements too. Typically, they are less obvious than the negative aspects because it's difficult to say anything good about a supposed enemy. But the ego acts as a neutralizing bridge between your body and your spirit. It's a necessary part of who you are. It tells us what is socially acceptable, and it's usually rational in decision-making, risk-assessing, and self-protecting. It tells you all about your earthly likes and dislikes and allows you to take pleasure in the 3D amusements of this world. Having a certain level of strength in ego means having a certain level of confidence. It's a valuable part of self-esteem.

We don't need to feel shame around feeling confident. We don't need to be ashamed of thinking we're great! (You *are* great!) The ego helps with this. We don't need to view the ego as our enemy. The more we can view it as a friendly acquaintance, the better off we will be. It's a lot easier to ride together in peace than to fight constantly with something that will always be there. We can coexist as long as we remember that the soul, not the ego, runs the show. Keeping the ego in check (and ignoring it when necessary) is key to finding balance.

If your ego is running the show, you haven't done anything wrong. You are not a bad person. The ego is supposed to be there, and you aren't doomed to be its servant forever. In fact, it's the other way around. Your soul's most powerful tool is using the ego to support you rather than bring you down. The mind is extremely powerful, and it will fast-track what you instruct it to believe. You can instruct it to be on your side and help you instead of letting it tear you down. It begins when you start to observe your ego. Then you can identify its patterns and triggers. Once you observe and befriend your ego, you will see that it's often predictable. You can use this to your advantage by recognizing what's happening before it starts to drag you into a dangerous downward spiral. Remember, you are not your ego. You can hear what it's saying without being invested in it. When you can take a step back and observe your thoughts, you realize that your thoughts are not you, for who would be the observer then? That's right, you guessed it, the soul—your higher consciousness. The ego practice is about learning to be centered from this place instead of the mind.

Transformation

If you think about it, ego death wouldn't be very enjoyable, would it? Not having an ego would be like showing up at the airport, paying for the ticket, and then deciding you have no interest in the destination. It would be a denial and disconnect from an integral part of our time here. Our souls understand we will inhabit a human body. We understand that part of this embodiment means cohabiting with an ego-mind. That can be tricky. We know it will be, but it's not all bad. There are positive aspects of the ego we can work to transform for our highest good. For example, jealousy can be turned into curiosity and admiration, anger into compassion, and fear into love.

The purpose of transforming the ego into a friend is to live a life in alignment as your most authentic self and with your highest good. It's possible to rewire your stories, and therefore rewire your mind. How? Let me share my perspective with you as an example. From time to time, if I'm not being a careful observer, I can let myself be convinced that some of my ego's stories are true. When that happens, I allow myself to be a victim of my stories. I used to view myself as damaged, broken, unrepairable, and incapable of success because of some of these stories. My ego would tell me that "You can't do this or that," or I'd think, "Who am I to want to do that?" My ego had stockpiled tons of evidence that showed why I was a failure with no future. It seemed like everyone around me was doing better than I was in some way. While it's a common experience to feel jealous, inadequate, or less-than, it doesn't lead anywhere productive. How much time have you spent on self-judgment and criticism? Hours? Years? Your whole life? We are our own worst critics, as the saying goes. When I realized, finally, that I had been doing this—and for way too long, I beat myself up over it! The guilt. The irony. It doesn't have to be like that.

Luckily, our ego stories are not set in stone. When we recognize when our ego is in control, then we can pause, forgive ourselves, and make a change. Scientists used to believe that the brain was unchangeable in adulthood. We now know that the brain can adapt and form new neural connections at any age. It's pretty remarkable. We can use this knowledge to our advantage by rewriting the stories of the ego—with permanent results. It can be accomplished in multiple ways, but perhaps one of the most accessible is writing, reciting, or listening to affirmations. Through this method, ingrained, negative neural pathways dissolve, and new, positive ones develop. It is an incredibly healing process. Personally, it made me realize that I didn't have to subscribe to these stories anymore, no matter how "true" I thought they were. Here are a couple of examples of my negative, old ego stories that I have since rewritten into supportive ones:

Ego Story: I have nothing to offer in the world, so I don't matter.

Became: I matter simply because I am here, and I add value by shining my light in whatever I do.

Ego Story: I need to make more money so I will be happier.

Became: I am abundant in many ways, and I can be happy right now.

Ego Story: I hate my job, and I'm wasting my life at it.

Became: I am helping others every day through small actions, even if I can't see the big picture.

Ego Story: My face wrinkles make me look old, and I need to lose weight to be beautiful.

Became: I don't need to change anything about my appearance to know that I am perfect and beautiful exactly as I am right now.

Ego Story: I haven't accomplished anything in life, and I don't have a purpose.

Became: Life is a journey to be enjoyed. My purpose is to shine as my unique self.

Ego Story: I should make myself as small as possible in the world to protect myself against judgment and rejection.

Became: I am welcome to shine my light. It is safe to be seen, heard, and to take up space.

I encourage you to look at your own recurring negative stories and rewrite them. Which ones keep coming up for you over and over again? How do you talk to yourself about yourself on a regular basis? Is the ego voice in your head nice to you? Or do you speak negatively about your body, your feelings, or your life? Ask yourself, "Do I want to align to negativity or possibility?" You get to choose your path here. It's never too late to rewrite and rewire—and science backs this up.

Depending on the severity of your stories and the strength of your ego voice, it might not be as quick as flipping a switch, but that doesn't mean it has to be difficult. Although initially, rewriting can bring up resistance, the more you practice, the less resistance there will be. The ego will say, "Oh, no, no, no. How dare you try to discount the things you know to be true? You can't believe this, right?" Feelings of resistance usually stem from a fear of the unknown. The negativity that we know also happens to be safe because it is familiar. We don't know what the future version of ourselves might feel like. In this process, we might worry about losing ourselves and not knowing who we are. Whenever a negative ego story starts to creep in, catch it and replace it with the rewritten story. Over time your old story will lose the strong meaning it once had and the new one will feel more true.

To identify as the old labels or stories is a sticky place. Kind of like those peel-and-stick nametags, except that instead of writing your name on them, you write your limiting beliefs, negative labels, and traumas. If you stick these to yourself enough times, you start to mistake them for your real identity. Someone who has spent most of their life in pain might not be able to see who they are because this pain defines them. It's what they know most about themselves—it's their identity. Naturally, trying to strip this away can be scary. "Who will I be without my main label?" There is an element of "fake it until you make it" here. But if it feels impossible, try rewriting to simply being open to the idea of something different. For example, if your ego story is that "money is evil," and there's no way you can suddenly believe that "I am worthy of millions of dollars," instead try, "I am open to the idea that money can be good, and I am worthy of having it."

These stories often run deep into the subconscious mind and bringing them to the surface is the first step in reversing them. The more you repeat your rewritten stories, the more you rewire your brain to believe them. As time goes on, they can continue to be rewritten to match your level of receptibility. It can take time, so don't be disappointed if you do this exercise and don't notice an instant change. Keep at it. The mind has to learn how to take a back seat here, and it *will* learn.

Living without your labels means not being a victim to them anymore and no longer placing blame on your body or anyone or anything else. I am *not* suggesting discounting a medical diagnosis or treatment, but I am suggesting that you look closely at how you choose to see your issues and that you don't identify *as* them. What if traumas, illnesses, and hardships could be teachers? Acknowledge their existence, and then lovingly release their hold on you. *See it to free it.*

From this perspective, we can begin to see past the victim mentality and identify opportunities to help others overcome the same things we struggle with. No one is born with self-doubt and limiting beliefs. These were learned at some point, and they can be unlearned. Thoughts are not tangible and set in stone; they are malleable. You hold the power to change them into thoughts that support you and that express love, safety, and abundance.

Ask yourself, objectively and without judgment, these questions:

- *What labels do I place on myself?*
- *How would it feel to peel off these sticky labels? Freeing or scary? Why?*
- *Am I open to a new way of thinking and identifying?*

Changing Fear into Love

Part of being an awakened soul is being able to see the difference between soul and ego. You are as the Universe created you; you are not what the ego says you are. Love is your natural state, and fear is the ego. As previously discussed, the ego comes with the mind, and the mind is part of being a human. It is not really you. The real you is the love of the Universe.

Essentially, the entire purpose of befriending your ego is so you can transform its fear-based narratives into ones of love. What is fear? Fear can manifest as anger, jealousy, worry, etc. There are some great acronyms for fear that act as a reminder to see it differently. A popular one is *False Evidence Appearing Real*, but my favorite is *Forgetting Everything's All Right*. The first one reminds us that our minds run wild and make up stories that aren't true. The second one reminds us that all is well, even when we don't feel like it is. Right now, at this moment, you are okay. Releasing fear means staying open to any and all possibilities. Staying open expands your receptivity for goodness.

I am often asked how to determine whether the voice we hear in our heads is ego or soul. If the thoughts are fear-based, then it's the ego. If the thoughts are rooted in love, then it's the soul. When it comes to connecting with other people's thoughts, meet their fear with love. If a friend complains to you, listen. Be supportive. But then meet their fear with love instead of more fear. Don't go down the spiral with them; that will drag your energy down too.

Living from a place of love might be the opposite of what feels natural to you because the world we live in is ruled by fear. We don't want to stray too far from what society deems acceptable for fear of being outcast or labeled. In essence, fear is what holds the rules of society in place. We all know the repercussions of not falling in line—being judged or rejected, experiencing monetary hardships, or facing emotional or personal challenges in our relationships. If we don't fall in line because we don't go out and get a job like we're "supposed to." The consequence? No money to live on, followed by hunger or homelessness. Or maybe our physical appearance doesn't meet the cultural standard of what it means to be "beautiful." The consequence? We might feel like we need to change ourselves by wearing a lot of makeup, doing excess exercise, or even having cosmetic procedures.

So, traditionally, we strive to have, do, and be the things society says we should have, do, and be --- all out of fear. We stay in line, whether that's due to fear of the consequences or fear of the unknown. The outside world says that you are your body and its accomplishments, that these things should be a certain way or fit into a specific box. But this is a collective illusion that humans have agreed to over time. What you see around you is all made up. Generation after generation, we keep the illusion alive, because well, "that's just the way it is."

Since we all believe in upholding society's rules (to some extent), when we fit into the world's expectation mold, we're promised acceptance and validation from others. But we end up denying our true selves while chasing the goals of a warped reality. Even though we feel like we've done everything we were supposed to do, we feel empty. More and more of us no longer wish to continue propping up the illusion by becoming attached to it. Our adherence to it creates a blockage between us, our higher self, and our highest good. This concept of "fitting in" is causing so much of the collective unhappiness in the world today. But we can wake up. We can recognize the illusion and live life on our own terms. We can make a change, and we can be free. The more of us that choose this, the more the traditional model starts to crumble.

To be free means to dismantle what you've always known to be real and to see it for what it is: *illusion*. To be free is to recognize yourself as the magical soul you are. To be free is to accept yourself for who you are, to make choices in alignment with your highest good, and to live from love. The more of us who decide for freedom, the more we shift these illusions, and eventually, the more the world might look very different.

Loving Yourself and Others

As we've seen, the ego naturally likes to tear us down, not lift us up. Sure, on the extreme opposite end, it might say, "You're the greatest, the best thing on this planet." This is also not a healthy ego response (again, it's a defense mechanism). The healthy ego that is balanced with the soul won't see you as better or worse than anyone else. To break the patterns we have engrained in our minds about ourselves, we must continue to relearn our thought patterns. As we relearn, we befriend our ego. When we befriend the ego, we decide to no longer be its victim and not be a victim of the world in general. Remember, you have control over yourself and your life. Repeat after me:

I am awesome.
I am a light in this world.
I am beautiful exactly as I am right now.
I am living life effortlessly.
I am in the flow of the Universe.
I am worthy of anything and everything I desire.

Changing negative talk into positive talk starts with you. Waiting around for other people to affirm to us what we want to hear only leads to disappointment or empty validation. We can be our own cheerleaders and the heroes of our stories.

*

These days, I *love* watching and celebrating other people's joys and successes. It makes me genuinely happy to be happy for others, and it reminds me that I am capable of the same. We all are.

After two years at my first corporate job, the team I was on started to fall apart because of the company's structural changes. That was the day I learned what the phrase "corporate reorganization" meant. One by one, employees left the company, and soon it was a mass exodus. There were just a handful of people left, including a middle-aged female colleague and me. We both wanted out too, not just because leaving was popular, but because, frankly, people were leaving for a reason. We'd talk every day, and she'd tell me about all the interviews she was getting. I, on the other hand, hadn't had a single one, and not for lack of trying. One day, she approached me, smiling from ear to ear. "I got a job offer!" Initially, I felt jealous. What was wrong with me? I hadn't had any interviews, much less an offer. My ego immediately tried to make the whole thing about me. My jealousy and doubt in myself blocked me from receiving what I wanted.

I didn't like that I felt jealous; it seemed childish and made me feel bad. I liked this coworker; I wanted her to be happy. So, while she worked her last two weeks at this job, I practiced being genuinely happy for her. I helped her count down the remaining days and talked with her about what her next chapter would look like. Her excitement was contagious. I was truly *feeling* happy for her. Within a matter of days, I got an interview and ended up getting the job, all on the first try (I thought at the time that this was a miracle). My shift in perspective allowed me not only to celebrate someone else's achievement but also to see what I was capable of, too, through sharing that uplifting energy. By feeling celebratory (instead of jealousy), I had raised my vibration, which allowed me to be receptive to what I wanted—and that was the true miracle.

When we celebrate others, the good energetic frequency that has blessed them will bless us too. We step into that same energy of joy when we genuinely share it. Lifting one another up benefits everyone's highest good—the last thing we need is more jealousy and anger in this world. Celebrating each other raises the vibration of the planet. It's truly a win-win situation.

THE MYSTERY

Why We Don't Know Everything

The Universe is under no obligation to make sense to you.

—Neil deGrasse Tyson

We Don't Have All the Answers

Our human minds want to understand everything and have answers to all our unknowns. Seeking understanding is what led me down this path, after all. The mind naturally wants to assign meaning to everything—it's human nature to wonder and to want to know. Understanding (or the perceived understanding) of our world gives us a sense of safety. We fear what we don't understand. The truth is, there are things we are not supposed to know. That doesn't mean we won't uncover more answers. It means that right now, in this time we live in, what we know is what we are ready to know. As we continue in our collective evolution, more will be revealed.

Part of our journey here is trusting in our faith in the Universe, surrendering to the mystery of this life. As much as we want to unveil the whole mystery, we're not meant to know, for whatever reason. We don't need to understand everything. If we did, we would. The human mind asks, "How? Why? When?" The soul answers, "It doesn't matter." How, why, and when are questions of the human ego. Even if someone (or some being or entity) were to explain it all to us, our human mind probably wouldn't comprehend it—it would be like hearing a concept clarified in a language you don't speak.

So, some of the things we consider mysterious may not be unknowable. We are just not capable of understanding them at this time. To explain them would be pointless and confusing. At this point in our evolution, we know all we need to know. The soul knows, so it doesn't need to ask. To make peace with that concept is to trust that everything is as it's supposed to be. As we continue to level up in our humanness, we increase our ability to receive additional information. The more open we are to receive, the more we can accept what is there for us.

It's a matter of receptivity. Receptivity comes with time and growth, which is what we are all doing together on this Earth. We are learning how to open ourselves up to receive the abundance of the Universe that is our birthright. We commit to this human construct of time in which our human selves grow and expand over a number of years. Every day, more and more of us become awakened. As an awakened soul, you are never too small to make a difference. You make a big difference. You are important.

To trust in the flow of life, most of us (me included) want proof that everything is going to be okay. But it works in the opposite way. Trust, and you'll find proof. What a boring life it would be if we all knew our destiny and how everything would unfold in our life plan. If we could speak to a younger version of ourselves and reveal all the things that have happened between then and now, that would ruin all their wonder, adventure, and anticipation. We don't know what tomorrow holds, and that's intentional. If we could see the trajectory of our lives unfold before us, we would become passive. We'd sit back and let life happen to us instead of taking action and being the drivers of our destinies. That mindset would deprive us of our necessary expansion. If we knew the outcome of all the events in our lives, how would we expand through experience?

There is a fair amount of trust and faith involved in this journey. Every individual will have to decide for themselves what is true for them. For me, it is an inner knowing that feels like a warm hug or like being home. I can breathe easier knowing that I am part of something bigger and always supported in this journey. I trust that we are divinely guided at all times. We don't know what's beyond where we stand or what lies ahead. What we might perceive as a setback on our path could be a shortcut, and when we finally get an overview of our life from our soul's perspective, we will feel gratitude for all the great and not-so-great moments because we'll see the bigger picture. It will all make perfect sense.

A Course in Miracles says, "Let all things be exactly as they are." We're not here to be tested. There are no right ways, right answers, wrong ways, or wrong answers. The way you undertake your journey is perfect for you, so enjoy the mystery of what might come next! Whenever you feel uncertain, try leaning upward into the space of surrender. Release and surrender create space for light, expansion, love, joy, and miracles.

We take part in decisions (like our soul plan and our free will choices), and there are decisions of which we are not a part. When it comes to our physical universe, there are many unanswered questions. "Why does the Universe exist in the first place? Where did it come from, and where is it going?" We don't have definitive answers, so, for now, we'll have to enjoy the mystery. Just as if a magic trick is revealed, it loses its wonder and allure; some unknowns keep us guessing and dreaming on purpose.

When it comes to healing, sometimes things just don't make sense. We can't (or we aren't supposed to) know the intricacies of certain situations. The Universe works in mysterious ways, and sometimes we don't know why things happen the way they do. What could be healed through a particular situation might not be apparent to us at the moment of it.

Life is not linear. The journey is not linear. When it seems like you've taken two steps backward, how can you be sure it wasn't two steps forward? We can't see the big picture, and we might not know at the moment.

Imperfection Is Beautiful

We don't need to feel "less than" if we don't have every answer or because we are imperfect beings in an imperfect world. It's all okay, really it is. There is beauty in imperfection. The more we practice returning to our truths, the easier it becomes over time to recenter to our knowing that we are divine. We all face moments of struggle. Every time (okay, most times) I throw myself a pity party, I get out my phone and I call an Uber to get me out of there. I'm getting better and better at being my own friend and looking out for myself when it's time to leave the pity party. The more we practice remembering, the more we increase our knowing and understanding, and the more rooted we become in our truths.

We are all just doing the best we can. Part of doing the best we can is accepting ourselves and others as we are. We are here to claim the energy of who we are now and who we came here to be!

There is a gift in imperfection: you can choose your path! You can adopt a new way of looking at life and create a new way of living. If I can go from wishing I had never been born to teaching other people how to transcend the madness of human life; anyone can. There is no reason why you can't have this transformation too.

Radical self-acceptance (including all your so-called imperfections) is essential to healing. When we learn to accept and love ourselves unconditionally, exactly as we are, we heal ourselves. A journey is rarely linear. There will be times you perceive as setbacks, but it is all part of the process. Remember, be kind and gentle with yourself. Life is not a race. There is no rush. Your journey is unique, and it's unfolding in perfect order. Trust in this.

EPILOGUE

Life is a journey to experiencing your true greatness so you can live fully every day of your life. You can achieve enlightenment—it's not reserved for the Buddha or enlightened monks. Enlightenment means "to be in the light." To remember that you are the light means you are enlightened.

You've already begun healing work. Now you know who you are. Now you know how you got here. Now you know what you're here for. Let's recap everything you've always wanted to know about life as a human being:

You are a soul in a body.
Your soul is a piece of the Universe itself.
The Universe is divinely perfect; therefore, you are divinely perfect.

You are love, and you are so loved.

You are a soul having a human experience, not a human having a spiritual experience.

You are here because you chose to be here.

You are here to live entirely in humanness from a soul-centered place.

You came to experience 3D enjoyment.

You are never alone. Support and guidance are always available to you.

Ask for signs and develop a relationship with your guides.

Ask for a miracle. Miracles are your right.

You matter. You are unique, and you are worthy and important.

Stay in curiosity and excitement with all things.

Your purpose is to express yourself and shine your unique energy into the world.

Success does not require suffering and sacrifice.

You are not here to be punished.

Befriend your ego, and you will take away its power over your life.

The healing journey is not linear.
Surrender and trust that the Universe is always looking out for you.
You get to choose what you think, what you say, and what you create.
You have infinite potential and possibilities available to you.
Let go of what's no longer serving you, and you will find freedom.
Fear is just a reminder to choose love.
Don't resist, don't cling, just let it all be as it is.
There are some things that we are just not meant to know.
Spirituality is a lifelong practice with no need to rush.
Healing yourself heals others.

Hopefully, you will not think the same way you did before you read this book. We are all in this together. I care about you and your journey. I care about making it as easy as possible for you to start the journey—and stay on the journey.

It is my sincere hope that after reading this book, you will recognize the love that you are and how much you matter. Your life is an exciting adventure to behold. Living it as your most authentic self means making choices in alignment with how you want to experience it. Choose love. Choose fun. Remember that you are exactly where you're supposed to be. When we continue to show up for ourselves and our healing, we show others that they are capable of doing the same. When we heal ourselves, we heal others. When we raise our own vibration, it contributes to the vibration of the world and raises the collective vibration for the benefit of all.

You are amazing, a wonder to behold. You deserve everything good that the Universe has to offer. This is your one and only shot at life in this body. I honor your light.

Now get out there and shine.

ACKNOWLEDGMENTS

I'm eternally grateful to everyone who played a part in bringing this book to life.

My gratitude goes out to all the teachers and healers who came before me.

A special big thanks to my personal coaches, guides, and healers—especially Robin Hallett.

I thank my husband, Sascha. I'm so glad we're partners in this wild human life journey.

To my parents, I'm so appreciative of your never-ending love. Thank you for always telling me I could do anything I wanted to.

Many thanks to my wonderful editor, Michael Ireland.

To Kristen Wise and Maira Pedierra at PRESStinely, thank you for guiding me through this process.

Most of all, this is for you, the reader. From the bottom of my heart, I thank you.

REFERENCES

A Course in Miracles. Huntington Station, NY: Foundation for Inner Peace, 1975. Print.

Bernstein, Gabrielle. https://gabbybernstein.com/new-blog-super-soul-sessions-talk-5-steps-spiritu-al-surrender/

Coelho, Paulo. *The Alchemist.* San Francisco: HarperSanFrancisco, 1998. Digital.

Einstein, Albert. https://www.brainyquote.com/quotes/albert_einstein_100298

Hallett, Robin. https://www.robinhallett.com/rock-star-readings/resistance-is-fultile-were-here-for-tangible-joy/

Newton, Michael. *Journey of Souls.* Minnesota, U.S.: Llewellyn Publications, 2002. Digital.

Rumi. https://quotefancy.com/quote/1320/Rumi-Stop-acting-so-small-You-are-the-universe-in-ecstatic-motion, https://www.outofstress.com/what-you-seek-is-seeking-you-rumi/

Selig, Paul. *The Book of Truth: The Mastery Trilogy.* New York: Penguin Publishing Group, 2017. Digital.

Tolle, Eckhart. *The Power of Now.* Vancouver, B.C., Novato, CA: Namaste Publishing, 2004. Print.

Tyson, Neil DeGrasse. *Astrophysics for People in a Hurry.* New York: W. W. Norton & Company, 2017. Digital.

To connect with Anna and continue your healing journey,
visit: annaschlinghoff.com.

Made in the USA
Las Vegas, NV
03 April 2023